Clash of Empires:
The British, French & Indian War
1754 – 1763

CLASH OF EMPIRES

THE BRITISH, FRENCH & INDIAN WAR
1754~1763

BY R.S. STEPHENSON

SENATOR JOHN HEINZ PITTSBURGH REGIONAL HISTORY CENTER

THIS PUBLICATION FUNDED THROUGH THE GENEROSITY OF
MELLON FINANCIAL CORPORATION

Updated 2006

Published by the Senator John Heinz Pittsburgh Regional History Center
An imprint of the Historical Society of Western Pennsylvania
1212 Smallman Street
Pittsburgh, PA 15222
(412) 454-6000
www.pghhistory.org

Printed in the United States of America

10 9 8 7 6 5 4 3 2

A special edition of *Western Pennsylvania History* magazine
Spring/Summer 2005, Volume 88, Numbers 1 & 2
Editor: Brian Butko
Editorial Assistant: Sherrie Flick
Project Associate: Lauren Uhl
Museum Assistant: Jamie Pennisi
Design: Quest Fore, Inc., Pittsburgh, Pa.

Western Pennsylvania History (ISSN 1525-4755) is published quarterly as a benefit of membership in the Historical Society of Western Pennsylvania, 1212 Smallman Street, Pittsburgh, PA 15222-4200. Institutional only subscription: $30: International, $35. • Periodicals postage paid at Pittsburgh, PA. Postmaster, send address changes to development, Historical Society of Western Pennsylvania, 1212 Smallman Street, Pittsburgh, PA 15222-4200. USPS 679-200. Formerly *Pittsburgh History.* • This publication is made possible, in part, by the Kenneth B. and Verna H. Haas bequest. A portion of the Historical Society's general operating funds is provided by the Allegheny Regional Asset District and the Pennsylvania Historical and Museum Commission.

Front cover: *General Johnson Saving a Wounded French Officer from a Tomahawk of a North American Indian*, c. 1764-68, by Benjamin West, (1738-1820), Derby Museums and Art Gallery, Derby, UK. West's monumental work commemorates an incident in the 1759 British siege of French Fort Niagara. It is one of the few period works that include representations of the three major players engaged in the struggle for North America.

Library of Congress Cataloging-in-Publication Data

Stephenson, R. Scott.
Clash of empires : the British, French, and Indian War, 1754-1763 / R.S. Stephenson. — 1st ed.
p. cm.
Includes index.
ISBN 0-936340-13-4
1. United States — History — French and Indian War, 1755-1763 — Exhibitions. I. Title.
E199.S827 2005
973.2'6 — dc22

2005007111

Contents

Acknowledgments

Like the French and Indian War, *Clash of Empires* began inauspiciously, took unexpected turns, and involved a large and diverse cast of characters. A boyhood visit to Fort Necessity National Battlefield sparked my interest. The challenging work of preserving and interpreting historic sites related to the conflict has been advanced by French and Indian War 250, Inc., led by Laura Fisher. Among the scholars with whom I have served in the national commemoration effort, Fred Anderson, Drew Cayton, and Dan Richter in particular have enriched *Clash of Empires.* The staff of the Canadian War Museum, particularly Peter Macleod, Tony Glenn, George Barnhill, and Mark Reed, have been exemplary partners. Darren Bonaparte, Karen Cooper, Michael Galban, Michelle Dean-Stock, Peter Jemison, Darwin John, Elmer John Jr., Walter John Jr., Don Secondine, Warren Skye, Gary Sundown, Lafayette Williams, Paul and Sue Winnie, and the American Indian core group from *The War That Made America* broadened my perspective. Monsieur Édouard Doucet, président, Société d'Histoire de Longueuil; Madame Marie-Paule Blasini, Archives Nationales, Aix-en Provence; Colonel Jean-Louis Travers, secrétaire de l'Association Musée du Génie; Colonel F. Dallemagne, président de l'Association Musée du Génie; Monsieur Jean-Marcel Humbert, conservateur général et directeur adjoint, Musée National de la Marine; Monsieur Didier Fontaine, Michel Cadieux, and Steve and Jacquie Delisle opened doors to the world of New France.

Many other colleagues have contributed generously to *Clash of Empires.* Colonial Williamsburg supported early research that led to this exhibit. Richard Guthrie, Alan Gutchess, Bob Connell, Jim Cawley, and Gerry Embleton deserve special mention. My thanks to all, as well as Joe Abeln, Joyce Adgate, Jessica Adler, The Dowager Countess of Albemarle, Sarah Allard, Cory Amsler, Terri Anderson, Barb Antel, Peter Argentine, Lynne Armstrong, John Astbury, Charles Aston Jr., Francis Back, Tessa Barber, Georgia Barnhill, Christina Bates, Barbara Bertucio, Jim Bishop, John Bittner, Rush Blady, Dede Blough, Lucie Boivin, Jeff Brock, Louise Brownell, Tom Bryant, Jarred Buba, Mike Burke, David Burnhauser, Barbara Carney, Alan Carswell, Nathan "Riff" Conner, Matt Conrad, Lynda Corcoran, Douglas Cortinovis, Travis Crowder, Jenine Culligan, Michael Dabrishus, Sylvie Dauphin, Sébastien Daviau, Nancy Davis, Catherine Dean, Timothy Decker, Ellen Doran, Susan Dreydoppel, Monica Dunham, Pat Dursi, Bruce Egli, Grace Eleazer, Anne Embleton, Kerry Falvey, Eric Ferris, Steven Fisher, Barbara Foster, Chris Fox, Marc Gadreau, Deborah Gage, Cecile Ganteaume, Tony Gerard, Grant Gerlich, Nick Gillis, Claudine Giroux, Robert Griffing, Leslie Grigsby, Marcia Grodsky, Jeff Groff, Bill and Penny Guthman, Tiffany Habay, Mary Lee Hagan, Jennifer, Sapata, Sasaya, and Logan Hamer-Pennisi, Sarah Hardy, Sue Hayward, Roland Hobbs, Caroline Hogan, Tom Hornbrook, Scott Houting, Lee Howard, Mark Hutter, Jill Iredale, Peter Jemison, Bob Johnson, Thad Kellstadt, Dan Kernen, Scott Kerschbaumer, Barbara Kessel, Nathan Kobuck, Alan Krause, Julia Kupina, Frederick Lapham, Franklin La Cava, Lara Lampenfield, Diane Le Brun, David Lezaro, Melissa Liles-Parris, Barbara Luck, Ken Mabrey, J. Robert Maguire, Richard Malley, Matthew Masich, Ted Masink, Stella Mason, Nadezhda Maykova, Moira McCaffrey, Dave McClanahan, Mary Jane McFadden, Jared McKenzie, Scot Meachum, Jill Meredith, Kathleen Werner Millward, Michael

Mitnick, Michael Montgomery, Michel Morrissette, Chris Muchow, Michael D. Myers, Patricia Nietfeld, Sam Pace, Louis Pfotenhauer, Gregoire Picher, Guy Plourde, David Pohl, Paul Prezzia, Margaret Pritchard, Jeffrey Ray, James Rees, Ally Reeves, Patrice Remillard, Nancy Richards, James B. Richardson III, Katherine Richmond, Graham Rimer, Mike Ripley, Betsy Robison, Phillip Rodenberg, Dorren Martin Ross, Pat Ruane, Linda Sanns, Erik Satrum, Susan Schoelwer, Duane Schrecengost, Rich Serafin, Julianne Simpson, Shaun Slifer, George Sluder, Betsy Solomon, John Somerville, Milla Springfeldt, Lynne Squilla, Sandy Streiff, Joe Steinmetz, Kathy Stocking, Denny Stone, Jesse Teitelbaum, Alicia Thomas, Fred Threlfall, Michael "Tent" Tolsen, Taresa Trembly, Michael Tuite, Mark Turdo, Carla Rosen Vacher, Christian Vachon, Guy Vadeboncoeur, Rachael Brodie Venart, Seth Waite, Tricia Walker, Ray Werner, Nick Westbrook, Peter Whitehouse, Jeanne Willoz-Egnor, Stephen Wood, Rochelle Dale, and Jan Zender. The list would double were my notes and memory more organized.

Clash of Empires is richer than it would have been but for the generosity of the private lenders who entrusted us with their treasures. They are listed on page 106. Thanks for kindnesses too numerous to recount.

Eisterhold Associates designed the *Clash of Empires* exhibition, and Jerry and Kate were gracious hosts on visits to Kansas City.

At the Senator John Heinz Pittsburgh Regional History Center, President and CEO Andrew E. Masich, Senior Vice President Betty Arenth, and Project Director David Halaas provided the opportunity to bring together artworks and objects from far-flung places. I am indebted to Museum Division Director Anne Madarasz, Exhibits Coordinator Ross Kronenbitter, and Project Associate Lauren Uhl. Brian Butko, Sherrie Flick, and Lora Hershey made this catalog possible. Research was facilitated by the Library & Archives staff, including David Grinnell, Art Louderback, and Kerin Shellenbarger. Erik Goldstein has been one of the most generous and enthusiastic supporters of *Clash of Empires* since the project began.

For efforts small and large, thanks to Virgil Albright, Sandra Baker, Sam Black, Carrie Blough, Frank Borbonus, Craig Britcher, Audrey Brourman, Brad Burmeister, Kevin Carhart, Ted Carpenter, Nick Ciotola, Meg Colafella, Niccole Cook-Atwell, Rob DeOrio, John Ford, Anne Fortescue, Anne Marie Grzybek, Naomi Horner, Linda Johnson, Courtney Keel, Bill Kindelan, Karen Lightell, Nancy Cain McCombe, Lori McElhattan, Michelle Pacis, Lorry Perkins, Mary Riethmiller, Jennie Rose, Ned Schano, John Shepherd, Tonia Suenkonis, Richard Stoner, Linda Tabit, Kathleen Wendell, John Weston, Tom White, Lisa Widmer, and the entire staff, volunteers, and interns at the History Center. David Scofield and Meadowcroft Museum staff assisted in the reconstruction and partial planned destruction of a section of Fort Necessity. No one worked harder to bring *Clash of Empires* together than my assistant Jamie Pennisi.

My parents, Robert and Judy Stephenson, made it possible for me to become a historian. My mother-in-law Judy Parfitt has been a godsend. Finally, my deepest love to Donna, Evans, and Ellie for remaining cheerful and patient for such a terribly long time. Yes, it's done.

Andrew E. Masich, President and CEO
David F. Halaas, Director of Library and Archives

Introduction

The war began in Western Pennsylvania and changed the world. Winston Churchill called it the first world war. In Europe, the French and British call it, rather unimaginatively, the Seven Years' War. French Canadians will always remember it as the War of the Conquest. Native people in North America have no name for the conflict, although it remains powerfully embedded in their collective consciousness as the last great war with the whites – one in which they held in their hands the balance of power and the destiny of a continent. Historians in the United States, for want of a better name, still refer to it as the French and Indian War.

But what's in a name? Plenty. The many names of this global war reflect the many peoples and voices caught up in the struggle. The war created the conditions that allowed the emergence of the American colonies into united states and world prominence.

At the break of dawn, May 28, 1754, in a rocky glen some 30 miles south of the strategic Forks of the Ohio, 22-year-old George Washington led his first command in a surprise attack on a party of French marines and Canadian militia. Things did not go as planned. The French were quickly overwhelmed and begged for quarter, but young Washington was in no position to give it. Instead, Tanaghrisson, his Seneca ally, seized the moment and determined the outcome of the fight. Before Washington could react, Tanaghrisson tomahawked the wounded French commander, Ensign Jumonville, a deliberate act calculated to force the British and French to war against each other. Only then, Tanaghrisson believed, would the Iroquois be able to consolidate their power over the tribes of the Ohio Country.

Washington looked on in horror, unable to prevent the slaughter of the French wounded. No war had yet been declared between France and England, but here in the dark woods of Western Pennsylvania, his Indian allies had forced the issue. This was no small firefight: the shots in Jumonville's Glen would echo around the world.

Winston Churchill's assessment was right — nearly a million people would die in the fighting that raged from North America to India and Asia, from Africa to Europe, and on all the seas between. To Europeans, the war was a centuries-old continuation of intermittent conflict between royal powers, especially arch-rivals England and France. That they would call the 1756-1763 conflict the Seven Years' War reflects their continental world view and entirely ignores the early fighting in North America, where, after all, the first shots were fired.

For Canadians, there was no doubt that the war was about the New World. Until 1763, France dominated the interior of the North American continent and more Native Americans spoke French than English. The British victory and the Treaty of Paris changed the world for French Canada, which became part of the British Empire. Those French settlers who remained behind struggled to retain their language, customs, and way of life. To them, this was a war of invasion and conquest.

For Indians, the war brought catastrophic consequences. No longer could they play European powers one against the other. Now forced to deal solely with the British and their American colonists, tribes were decimated by disease, famine, and war. The forced removal from ancestral homelands drastically changed tribal languages, traditions, and lifeways.

In the United States today, the war is all but forgotten, lost in the shadow of the American Revolution. The name "French and Indian War," or as most people know it, the war before the Revolution, reflects an ethnocentric view: the war we Anglo-Americans fought against our French and Indian enemies. This perspective ignores the role of Indians as allies and equals, instead casting them as inconsequential players in a world drama.

On the occasion of the 250th anniversary of the conflict, the Senator John Heinz Pittsburgh Regional History Center presents the exhibition, *Clash of Empires: The British, French, & Indian War, 1754-1763*, and this companion book drawn from the exhibit text, written by Project Curator R. Scott Stephenson, Ph.D. Both tell the compelling story of the three-way struggle for the possession and control of North America.

Chapter 1

An Expedition to Save New France

Early in 1753, nearly 2,000 French soldiers, Canadian militiamen, and Indian allies set out from Montreal on an arduous military campaign to the west. Their mission was to build a series of forts on *La Belle Riviere,* "the Beautiful River," known to English inhabitants and Iroquois Indians as the Ohio River (and, back to its source, the Allegheny). For many, it seemed that the very survival of New France rested on the outcome of this expedition.

New France was more than 150 years old in 1753. Quebec, the first permanent French settlement, had been founded just a year after Jamestown in Virginia. Most of the approximately 70,000 French-speaking inhabitants, along with several thousand enslaved Africans and American Indians, lived along the St. Lawrence River in Canada, but widely scattered settlements, religious missions, trading posts, and forts stretched from Isle Royale and Acadia on the north Atlantic coast to the Illinois country and Louisiana.

Adapting to Conditions

Travelers in New France used many objects and technologies borrowed from the native peoples of North America. One of the most useful items on a continent crisscrossed by rivers and lakes was the birch bark canoe. By the 1740s, canoes more than 30 feet long — paddled by a crew of eight to 10 men — carried as much as 5,000 pounds of cargo.

Canadians and French soldiers serving in the colony frequently adopted articles of Native American dress, including moccasins, leggings, and breechclouts that made travel easier. Snowshoes and wooden toboggans made it possible to move about the country in winter. Woven burden straps allowed heavy loads to be carried across road-less lands.

All Canadian males between the ages of 16 and 60 were enrolled in the militia company of their home parish or city neighborhood, creating a force of about 13,000 men in 1750. Militiamen were required to maintain arms and ammunition, train periodically (mostly by firing at targets), and turn out for unpaid military service when called upon. Those who had experience paddling canoes or fighting enemy Indians or English colonists were particularly prized for military campaigns. In addition to articles of Indian dress, such men often wore indelible marks of their experience among Native nations. "One recognizes them easily," a French officer later observed, "by their looks, by their size, and because all of them are tattooed on their bodies.... One would not pass for a man among the Indians of the Far West if he had not had himself tattooed."

New France could not exist without American Indian allies. Although both sides used the metaphor of a French "father" and his Indian "children" to describe their relationship, French officials knew they could not dictate the behavior of fiercely independent native peoples. Warriors from dozens of nations joined French campaigns against the British colonies, but they did so on their own terms and only when it appeared to be for the good of their people. Canada's staunchest native allies during the conflicts of the 18th century came from a confederation of seven villages in the St. Lawrence Valley. These communities, all of which were attended by Catholic missionaries, included Iroquois peoples (particularly Mohawks and Onondagas) as well as Abenakis, Hurons, Algonquins, and Nippissings.

The Ohio Expedition of 1753-54

The French fort-building expedition of 1753-54 was the last in a series of steps to prevent British colonial expansion across the Appalachian Mountains. Draining more than 200,000 square miles, the Ohio River provided easy access to the North American interior. British control of this strategic waterway would cut New France in half and give it the economic and military strength to threaten France itself. In the 1740s, British traders urged France's Indian allies to rebel, and land speculators eyed the Forks of the Ohio River, site of present-day Pittsburgh. French officials concluded that the only way to secure control of the region was to establish forts in the Ohio Valley.

By 1753, the population of New France was largely native-born. For generations, war had been more common than peace, and Canadian society had developed a strong military character. Most men had served on at least one campaign, and professional soldiers formed a large, visible part of society. Military service was an important career for the sons of prominent Canadian families.

European visitors were impressed by the Canadians' hardiness and military skill. The militia and colonial regulars of the *Troupes de la Marine*, who were recruited in France and led by mostly Canadian officers, mastered forest warfare tactics borrowed from their American Indian allies. These characteristics were key in defending New France against its powerful British rivals.

Outnumbered 20 to one by British colonists, New France relied heavily on military institutions and native alliances for its defense. The most numerous group in the Ohio expedition of 1753-54 was drawn from the Canadian militia. More than 1,000 militiamen were joined by several hundred colonial regulars of the *Troupes de la Marine*. About 5,000 of these troops were posted in Canada, Louisiana, and Isle Royale (Louisburg) at this time. Several hundred men from Indian communities in the St. Lawrence Valley also accompanied the Ohio expedition of 1753-54. These warriors were critical to the survival of New France, and colonial officials devoted considerable money and diplomatic efforts to maintain good relations.

Carte De L'Amerique Septentrionale Depuis le 28 Degré de Latitude jusqu'au 72 (Map of North America from 28 to 72 degree latitude), c. 1755
Jacques-Nicholas Bellin
Hand colored engraving, 53 x 84 cm
Library and Archives Canada
(NMC 21057)

New France consisted of settlements in Canada, the Illinois country, and Louisiana with most of the population concentrated in the St. Lawrence Valley between Montreal and Quebec. Dozens of trading posts and forts connected these settlements and facilitated trade and alliances with numerous Native American nations. An extensive web of navigable waterways allowed travelers to paddle from Quebec to New Orleans, and nearly as far west as the Rocky Mountains, with no more than a few short portages across land.

Le Marquis de la Galissonière (1693-1756), mid-18th century
Artist unknown
Oil on canvas, 67 x 36 inches
Stewart Museum, Montreal (Canada),
Photograph by Jasmin Provost

As acting governor of New France (1747-1749), la Galissonière tried to prevent the expansion of British influence in North America. He dispatched a military expedition to the Ohio Valley in 1749 and recommended building forts there, as well as sending French settlers and soldiers to strengthen posts from the Champlain Valley to the Illinois country.

To assert France's territorial claims to the Ohio Valley, Captain Pierre Joseph Céloron de Blainville buried a series of engraved lead plates as the expedition moved through the region. In the 1790s, a group of boys playing near the mouth of the Muskingum River in Ohio found this original lead plate from the expedition. Half of it was melted down for bullets before its significance was realized. Another Céloron plate was found along the Ohio River in 1848.

Céloron Plate, 1749
Artist unknown
Lead, 8 x 4-1/8 inches
American Antiquarian Society,
Worcester, Mass.

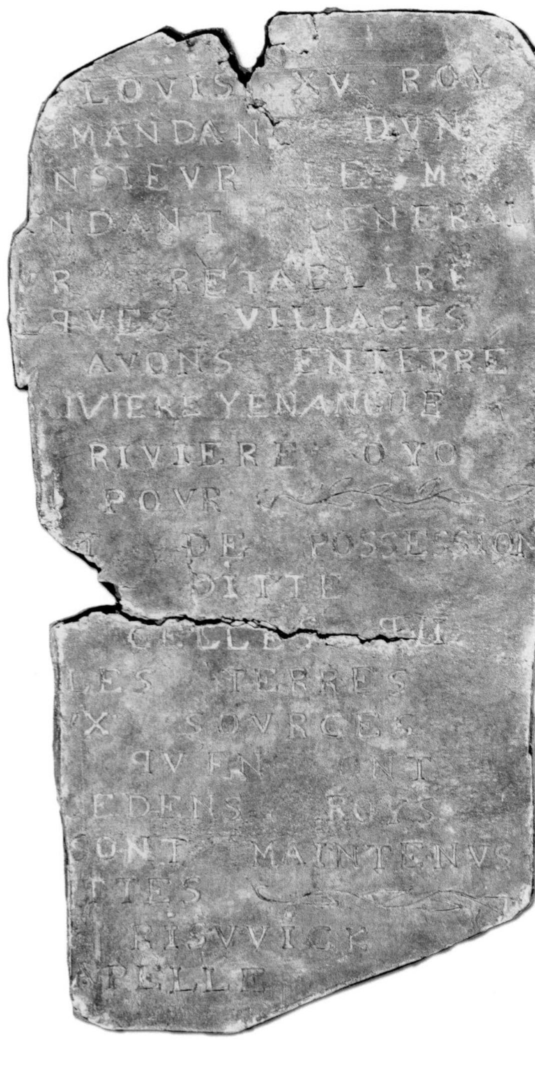

Charles-Jacques Le Moyne, 3e [sic]
Baron de Longueuil, c. 1740
Artist unknown
Oil on canvas, 76 x 63.3 cm
Collection Musée d'art de Joliette, long-term loan of Historical Society of Longueuil

This unsigned portrait is believed to depict Charles Le Moyne, 2d Baron de Longueuil (1687-1755), not the third as noted in its traditional title. Experts in 18th-century French military dress date the sitter's uniform to the 1730s. The image is therefore more likely to represent a 50-some-year-old 2d Baron than his son and successor, Charles-Jacques Le Moyne, who would have been a boy at the time this artwork was executed.

Le Moyne was a native Canadian officer in the colonial regulars or *Compagnies Franches de la Marine*. In 1739, he led the first French military expedition to descend the Ohio River, passing the future site of Pittsburgh. As acting governor of New France in 1752, he opposed the aggressive actions on the Ohio that sparked the outbreak of war.

Charles-Jacques Le Moyne, 3d Baron de Longueuil (1724-1755), c. 1753
Artist unknown
Oil on canvas, 76.4 x 61 cm
McCord Museum of Canadian History, Montreal, purchase from Ian Satow, (M985.219)

Marie-Catherine Fleury Deschambault (1740-1818), c. 1754
Artist unknown
Oil on canvas, 76.4 x 63.6 cm
Collection Musée d'art de Joliette, long-term loan of Historical Society of Longueuil

LIKE HIS FATHER, UNCLES, AND BROTHERS, Charles-Jacques Le Moyne entered the colonial regulars at an early age. He became part of the close-knit cadre of Canadian officers who defended New France through its final years. Upon his father's death in January 1755, Le Moyne became 3d Baron de Longueuil. He died in action later that year while serving with a contingent of Canadian Iroquois warriors against New England forces.

MARIE-CATHERINE-ANNE FLEURY DESCHAMBAULT married Charles Le Moyne, 3d Baron de Longueuil in January 1754, when she was just 13 years old. Like her fellow Canadians, Deschambault's life was transformed by the conflict that broke out that year, which left her widowed before the age of 16.

The Portage: An Iroquois Warrior and Canadian Militiaman at Presque Isle, 1753-54
Gerry Embleton, 2005
Photograph by Rob Long

All adult Canadian men were enrolled in the militia company of their home parish or city neighborhood. But New France could not have defended itself without American Indian allies, too. Warriors from dozens of nations joined French campaigns against the British colonies, though they did so on their own terms and only when it appeared to be for the good of their people.

Chapter 2

A People Between

The French expedition to the Ohio in 1753-54 entered the crossroads of 18th-century Native America. Depopulated in the 1600s by imported European diseases, intertribal warfare, and drought, the upper Ohio Valley became a rich hunting ground and refuge for displaced peoples during the half century before the French invasion.

The diverse groups who came to be known as "Ohio Indians" emigrated from across eastern North America. They included Lenapes, Munsees, and Shawnees from the Delaware Valley; Nanticokes from the Chesapeake; Mahicans from the Hudson Valley; Wyandots from near Detroit; and Iroquois families from as far away as the St. Lawrence Valley. All formed new communities in the region before 1753.

Most of these people shared the bitter experience of European colonial encroachment and dispossession, in some cases aided by the Iroquois Confederacy. All were prepared to defend tenaciously their independence in this new homeland.

Commercial Hunting

In the early 1700s, the Ohio Country was one of the richest hunting grounds in northeastern North America. Large populations of whitetail deer and fur-bearing animals like beaver and otter drew native hunters and their families from distant regions. These skins and furs were exchanged for European manufactured goods upon which many Indian peoples had come to depend. Demand for deerskins was particularly high in the British colonies. By 1753, Pennsylvania and Virginia-based traders carried textiles and clothing, firearms, ammunition, cooking utensils, and other goods across the Allegheny Mountains on horseback each year. Canadian merchants favored the more luxurious furs from northern lands but began sending canoes with trade goods to "the Beautiful River" around 1750.

The rivalry between British and French empires created many dangers for American Indians, but the Europeans' competition for allies also empowered native peoples to extract gifts and favorable terms of trade. By 1753, most eastern American Indians had had access to European manufactured goods for well over a century. Many groups became dependent on these supplies. The 18th-century "Indian Fashion" incorporated items that could only be obtained through exchange and gift-giving. Selectively adopting these manufactured goods, native peoples developed a rich style of dress, but one that still drew on traditional practices, ideas, and technology.

The struggle for American Indian sovereignty was waged in the council room as much as on the battlefield. Indian groups could play the British and French off one another. A decade before the 1753 Ohio expedition, an Iroquois leader had warned a Pennsylvania official

> they were not unacquainted with their own true Interests; and therefore would not join with either Nation [Britain or France] in the War, unless compelled to it for their own Preservation: That hitherto, from their Situation and Alliances, they had been courted by both; but should either prevail so far as to drive the other out of the Country, they should be no longer considered, Presents would be no longer made to them, and in the End they should be obliged to submit to such Laws, as the conquerors should think fit to impose on them.

The size and boldness of the French and Indian force that invaded the Ohio Valley in 1753 alarmed the residents, who met to consider a response. Opinions were divided, for some considered the French a useful ally against the British colonies, particularly Virginia. The greatest opposition to the French came from a Seneca chief named Tanaghrisson. Traveling from his home near the Forks of the Ohio (Pittsburgh) to the French camp at Presque Isle on Lake Erie, Tanaghrisson delivered a stern warning to the commander through a Canadian translator. He later recounted the speech for 21-year-old Virginia Major George Washington, who recorded it in his journal:

> Fathers, both You and the English are White. We live in a Country between, therefore the Land does not belong either to one or the other; but the GREAT BEING above allow'd it to be a Place of residence for us; so Fathers, I desire you to withdraw, as I have done our Brothers the English, for I will keep you at arms' length. I lay this down as a Tryal for both, to see which will have the greatest regard to it, & that Side we will stand by, & make equal sharers with us.

The French commander's reply was sharp and demeaning. Refusing to accept Tanaghrisson's message, he retorted, "I despise all the stupid things you said," and warned, "If there are any persons bold enough to set up barriers to hinder my march, I shall knock them over so vigorously that they may crush those who made them." Nine months later, it was Tanaghrisson who struck a dramatic blow against the French, sparking a conflict that would spread around the globe.

Lapowinsa, 1735
Gustavus Hesselius
Oil on canvas, 33 x 25 inches
Atwater Kent Museum of Philadelphia,
Historical Society of Pennsylvania Collection

Lapowinsa was among the Delaware Indians driven from their homes in the early 18th century. Many relocated to the Susquehanna Valley, while others joined their kinsmen in the Ohio Country, where Delaware settlements had been established as early as the 1720s.

Flintlock Firearm [British Trade Gun], c. 1760
Bumford Shop, London
Beech, iron, steel, paint, 62-1/2 inches
The Colonial Williamsburg Foundation, 1981-5

THIS IS A RARE INTACT EXAMPLE of the most common type of British trade gun produced for the North American market between the 1730s and the American Revolution. The relatively low quality of these guns may have contributed to the growing popularity of rifles among eastern American Indians during the era of the French and Indian War.

RIFLES (OFTEN CALLED RIFLE BARREL GUNS IN THE PERIOD) had spiral grooves cut into their iron barrels to spin the bullet for increased accuracy. Such weapons were popular not only with whites but with Delaware and Shawnee hunters who settled in the Ohio Country during the middle decades of the 18th century. This example is attributed to German-born gunsmith Johann Andreas Albrecht (1718-1802), a member of the Moravian Christian community in Pennsylvania. It was passed down through the family of Edward Marshall, a Pennsylvanian who participated in the 1737 Walking Purchase that drove Delaware Indians from their homelands.

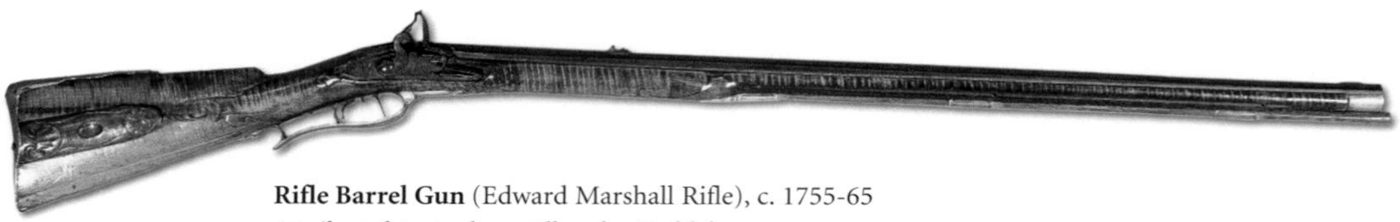

Rifle Barrel Gun (Edward Marshall Rifle), c. 1755-65
Attributed to Andreas Albrecht, Bethlehem or Christian Springs, Pa.
Curly maple, iron, brass, 52-3/4 inches
Mercer Museum of the Bucks County Historical Society, gift of Marshall Ridge, 1922, ACC 10780

Stone Smoking Pipe, mid-18th century
Northwestern Indiana or Michigan
Red catlinite, 2-1/4 x 1-1/8 inches
Collection of Steve Fuller

STONE SMOKING PIPES, often crafted from a distinctive red stone found in the midwest, were made by both Native American and Canadian artisans. The distinctive bowl shape may have inspired the colonial blacksmiths who fashioned the first pipe tomahawks.

EIGHTEENTH-CENTURY AMERICAN INDIANS were discerning customers, and European merchants eager to do business developed specialized goods to meet consumer demand. Combining a smoking pipe and trade axe, the pipe tomahawk appeared in Canada and Pennsylvania by the end of the 1740s and quickly grew in popularity during the French and Indian War.

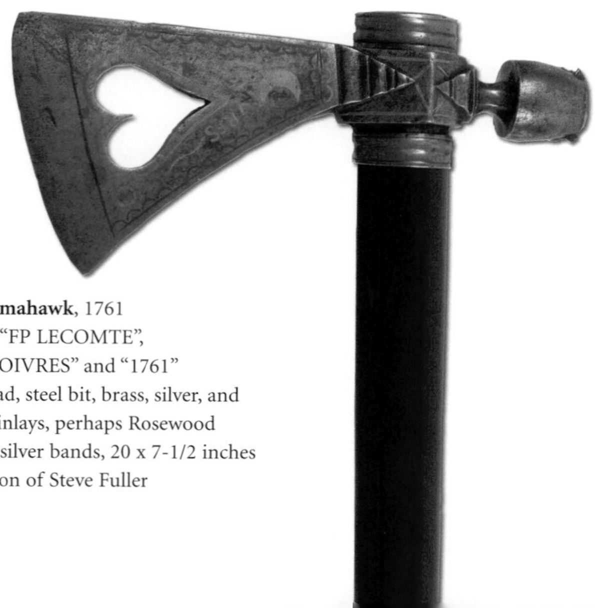

Pipe Tomahawk, 1761
Inlayed "FP LECOMTE",
"A. LEPOIVRES" and "1761"
Iron head, steel bit, brass, silver, and copper inlays, perhaps Rosewood handle, silver bands, 20 x 7-1/2 inches
Collection of Steve Fuller

By the mid-18th century, eastern American Indians with access to European manufactured goods developed distinctive styles of dress and decorative arts by creatively adapting imported garments, cloth, ribbon, glass beads, and other materials.

American Indian and family, 18th century [c. 1764]
Benjamin West, unsigned
Oil on canvas, 24 x 19 inches
Hunterian Collection, Hunterian Museum at the Royal College of Surgeons (RCSSC/P249)

Leggings, 18th century
Northeastern North America, likely Delaware
Deerskin, black-dyed, deer hair,
red-dyed, porcupine quills, metal cones,
77.7 x 40 x 29 cm; 84.1 x 36.8 x 22.9 cm
Livrustkammaren invnr 20643-44
(45/560 b), Stockholm, Sweden

Constructed from a smoked and dyed deerskin, these leggings, collected in the Delaware Valley, suggest the rich decorative possibilities achieved using natural materials even before imported European materials became available.

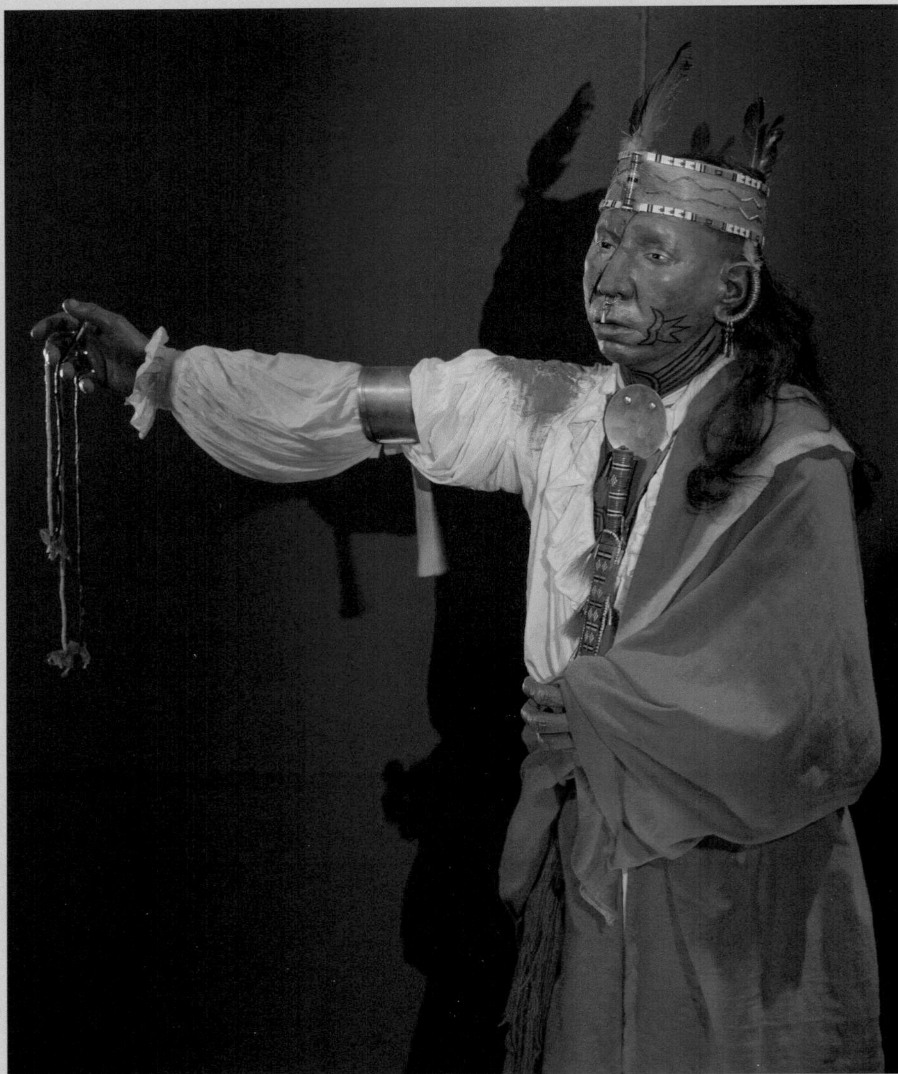

Tanaghrisson: An Ohio Iroquois Leader Warns the French, September 2, 1753
Gerry Embleton, 2005
Photograph by Rob Long

The most active opponents of the French expedition to build forts in the Ohio Country were the Ohio Iroquois leaders Scarouady, an Oneida also known as Monacatootha, and Tanaghrisson, a Seneca known to the British as "Half King." In September 1753, Tanaghrisson delivered a warning to the French commander at Fort Presque Isle on Lake Erie. Nine months later, he carried out his threat at a forested hilltop south of present-day Uniontown, Pennsylvania, that would come to be known as Jumonville Glen.

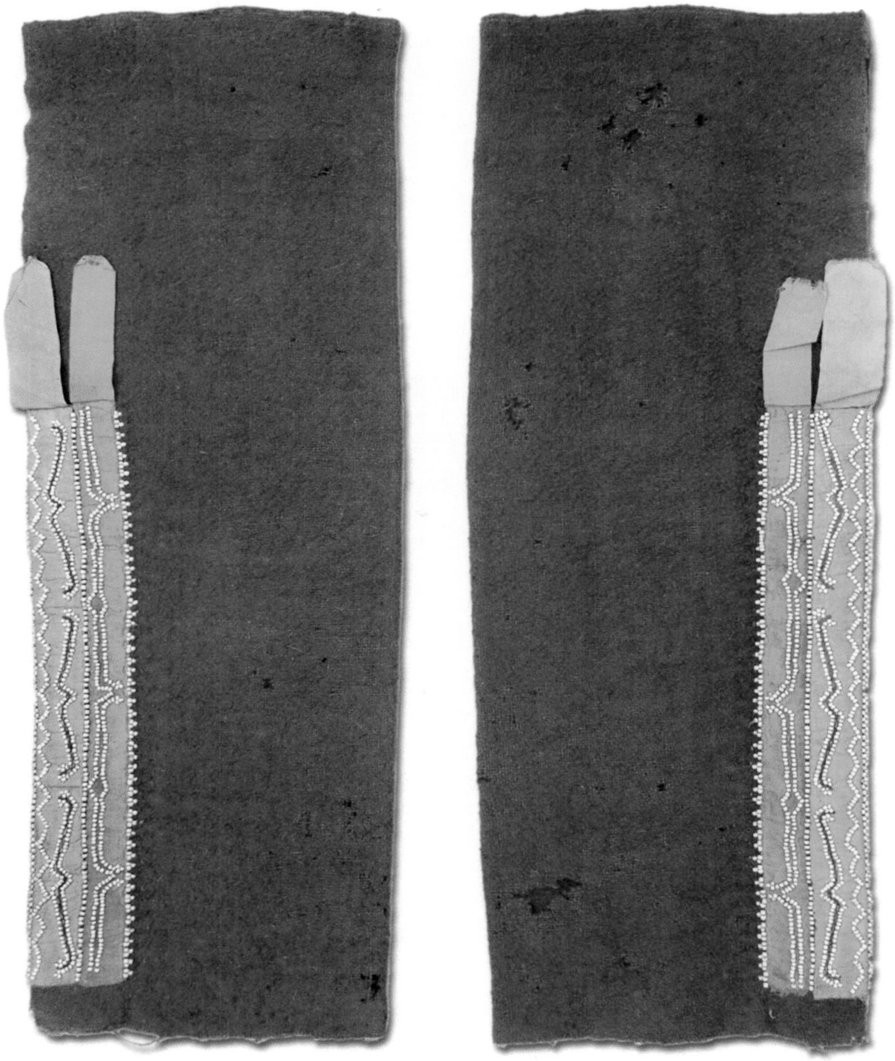

Green wool leggings with ribbon and bead decoration, mid-18th century
North-East North American
Wool, cotton, silk, glass beads,
60.5 x 22 cm
Peter the Great Museum of Anthropology and Ethnography (Kunstkamera) of the Russian Academy of Sciences, 1901-3A and 1901-3B,
Photograph by Shapiro Stanislav

EMBELLISHED WITH RIBBON EDGING AND GLASS BEADS, these tradecloth leggings offer an excellent example of how traditional garments and decorative ideas were rendered in new materials acquired through exchange with European traders.

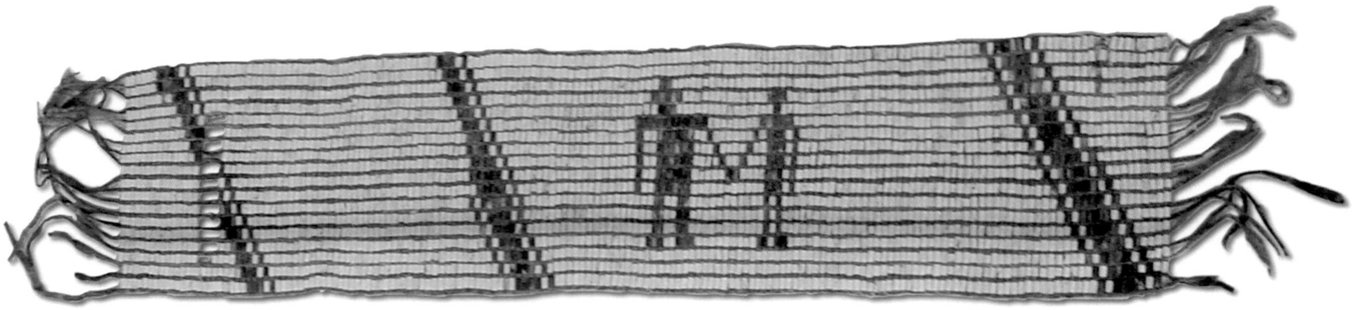

Wampum Belt, 17th or 18th century
Lenni-Lenape
Whelk and quahog shell beads, leather,
33-1/2 inches long x 5-3/4 to
5-7/8 inches wide
Atwater Kent Museum of Philadelphia,
Historical Society of Pennsylvania
Collection, HSP.1857.3

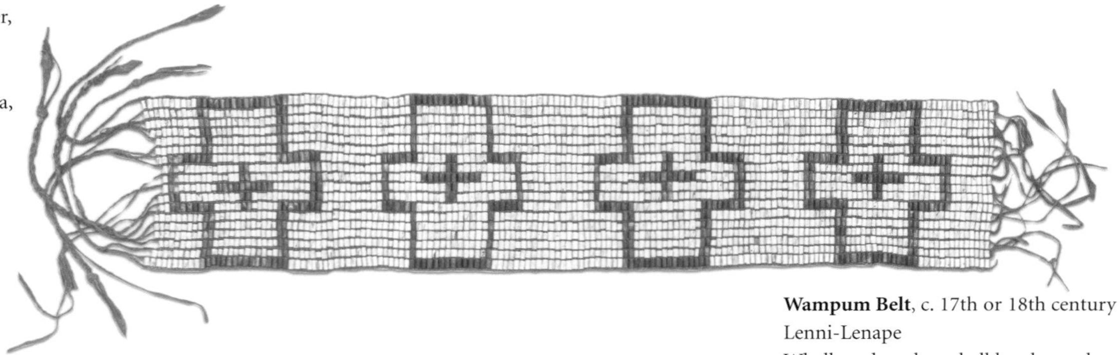

Wampum Belt, c. 17th or 18th century
Lenni-Lenape
Whelk and quahog shell beads, cordage,
42 x 5-5/57 inches
National Museum of the American
Indian, Smithsonian Institution,
Washington, D.C., photograph by
David Heald, 5/3150

BRITISH, FRENCH, AND AMERICAN INDIAN PEOPLES in much of eastern North America developed elaborate diplomatic rituals to guide their negotiations and agreements. The most important and widespread of these practices was the exchange of strings and woven belts of shell "wampum" beads. Wampum — a term from the language of Algonquian Indians in coastal New England — was applied in the 17th and 18th centuries to white and dark-purple beads fashioned from shells found in coastal waters as far south as New Jersey.

The use of wampum in intercultural diplomacy drew heavily from the traditions and practices of the Iroquois peoples. The strings and belts of wampum that were exchanged acted as credentials for the speakers and records of each point made or agreement reached. Wampum belts, which could reach six or more feet in length, often bore iconographic symbols intended to remind the speaker and viewers of the accompanying message.

By the 1750s, the exchange of wampum strings and belts had spread widely among British, French, and Indian peoples living east of the Mississippi Valley. The persistence of native forms of ritual in diplomatic exchanges among these groups reveals the decisive role native people played in the precariously shifting balance of power in North America. The wampum belts above are two of three that descended in the Penn family, proprietors of the colony of Pennsylvania from 1681 until the American Revolution. They have long been attributed to a 1682 treaty between founder William Penn and Delaware Indians near the site of Philadelphia.

During a visit to the Huron village of Lorette near Quebec City in 1750, Swedish naturalist Peter Kalm observed, "Many of the Indians wear a large French silver coin with the king's effigy on their breasts."

Medal, (Reign of Louis XV)
Jean DuVivier
Silver, 55 cm diameter
Front: LUDOVICUS XV REX CHRISTIANISSIMUS
Back: HONOS ET VIRTUS
Library and Archives Canada, Ottawa (PAC H1253)

British Peace Medal, early 18th century (Reign of George II)
English, private issue medal, engraver unknown
Brass, 1 inch diameter, excluding suspension loop
Collection of the Fort Ticonderoga Museum

Colonial officials in North America began issuing medals bearing the likenesses of British or French monarchs to American Indian leaders in the 1600s. Commonly known today as "peace medals," these decorations carried deep political significance, for acceptance and display of a medal was a sign of the bearer's loyalty. This example probably matches those presented to Ohio Indian leaders in 1754 at the behest of Virginia Governor Robert Dinwiddie.

Chapter 3

The Storm Rising in the West

Following the founding of Virginia in 1607, a string of British colonies developed along the Atlantic seaboard. Immigration and natural growth swelled the colonial population to more than 1.5 million by 1750, creating a constant demand for new agricultural land. Although most British colonists lived only a few days travel from the coast, colonial land holdings extended far into the North American interior. French and American Indian claims to those same lands made conflict inevitable.

By the end of the 1740s, British officials viewed with alarm the prospect of a French empire stretching uninterrupted from Canada to Louisiana. The riches that would flow to France could threaten the very existence of the British colonies, and perhaps Great Britain itself. British strategists believed expansion across the Appalachian Mountains was critical to the security and prosperity of Britain's Atlantic empire.

A Warning to the French

France and Britain were officially at peace in 1753. The last war between them had ended in 1748, but disputes over colonial boundaries remained. British officials viewed French activities from Acadia to the Ohio Valley as encroachments. Virginia Governor Robert Dinwiddie strongly advocated confronting the French. In 1749, Virginia land speculators of the newly formed Ohio Company obtained a land grant near the Forks of the Ohio River, but their plans to erect a fort and settlement there were threatened by Governor Duquesne's expedition from Canada. In October 1753, Dinwiddie and his council dispatched George Washington, a young militia officer, to gather intelligence and deliver a warning to the French commander on the Ohio.

When Major George Washington returned with confirmation of French intentions in January 1754, Governor Dinwiddie moved quickly to raise an army. This task was far more complicated in the British colonies than in New France. On paper, the Virginia militia alone (14,000 men) outnumbered its Canadian counterpart, but unlike the Canadians, the Virginia militia had not participated in a major military campaign for generations. Support from other British colonies was weak. With few Indian allies or British soldiers available for defense, Virginia and other colonies had, when the need arose, raised "provincial" troops for a limited term of service. Dinwiddie created such a regiment for the Ohio expedition, the first detachment of which set out in April under newly promoted Lieutenant Colonel Washington.

While the Virginians marched to the Forks of the Ohio, the French drove off an advance party of workers and began building Fort Duquesne. Washington was still 60 miles away when Seneca chief Tanaghrisson sent warning of an enemy party nearby. On the morning of May 28, 1754, Washington and 40 soldiers attacked Ensign Joseph Coulon de Villiers de Jumonville and his detachment of Canadian militia. The brief, chaotic firefight ended with the wounded Jumonville producing a written summons similar to the one Washington had carried to the French six months before. Tanaghrisson, whose demands that the French leave his country had been ignored and belittled, killed Jumonville with a blow from his tomahawk, saying, "thou art not yet dead, my Father."

Revenge at the Great Meadows

Expecting retaliation for his attack on Jumonville, Washington set his men to building a small fort at the nearby Great Meadows. This natural clearing in the heavily timbered Allegheny Mountains seemed "a charming field for an encounter" to the inexperienced Virginian, who expected a European-style battle in the open. His expectations were dashed on July 3, 1754, when Jumonville's brother, using the cover of the surrounding forest, attacked with 500 French soldiers and Canadian militiamen and 100 allied warriors. The action quickly settled into an uneven firefight, with bullets raining down on Fort Necessity from wooded hillsides nearby.

By evening, one-third of Washington's force was dead or wounded. Heavy thunderstorms and constant firing left most defenders' firearms useless. When his demoralized soldiers broke into the rum supply, Washington had little choice but to surrender. Washington's force was allowed to return to Virginia with the honors of war (arms, flags, and a symbolic piece of artillery), but a provision in the capitulation assigned Washington responsibility for the "assassination" of Ensign Jumonville. Washington and his officers blamed this seeming admission of culpability on poor translation, but the damage to Washington's reputation was deep. "I wish Washington had acted with prudence and circumspection requisite in an officer of his rank," New York Indian agent William Johnson complained. Washington's sometime-ally Tanaghrisson later complained that although he was a good-natured man, the young Virginian had little experience and "made no Fortifications at all, but that little thing upon the Meadow, where he thought the French would come up to him in open field."

Not surprisingly, the most damning criticism came from Canada. After the capitulation, Washington's campaign journal fell into French hands, and was eventually passed to Governor Duquesne, who observed, "He lies a great deal in order to justify the assassination of Sieur de Jumonville, which has recoiled upon him and which he was stupid enough to admit in his capitulation." Duquesne concluded, "There is nothing more unworthy, lower, or even blacker than the opinions and way of thinking of this Washington! It would have been a pleasure to read his outrageous journal to him right under his nose."

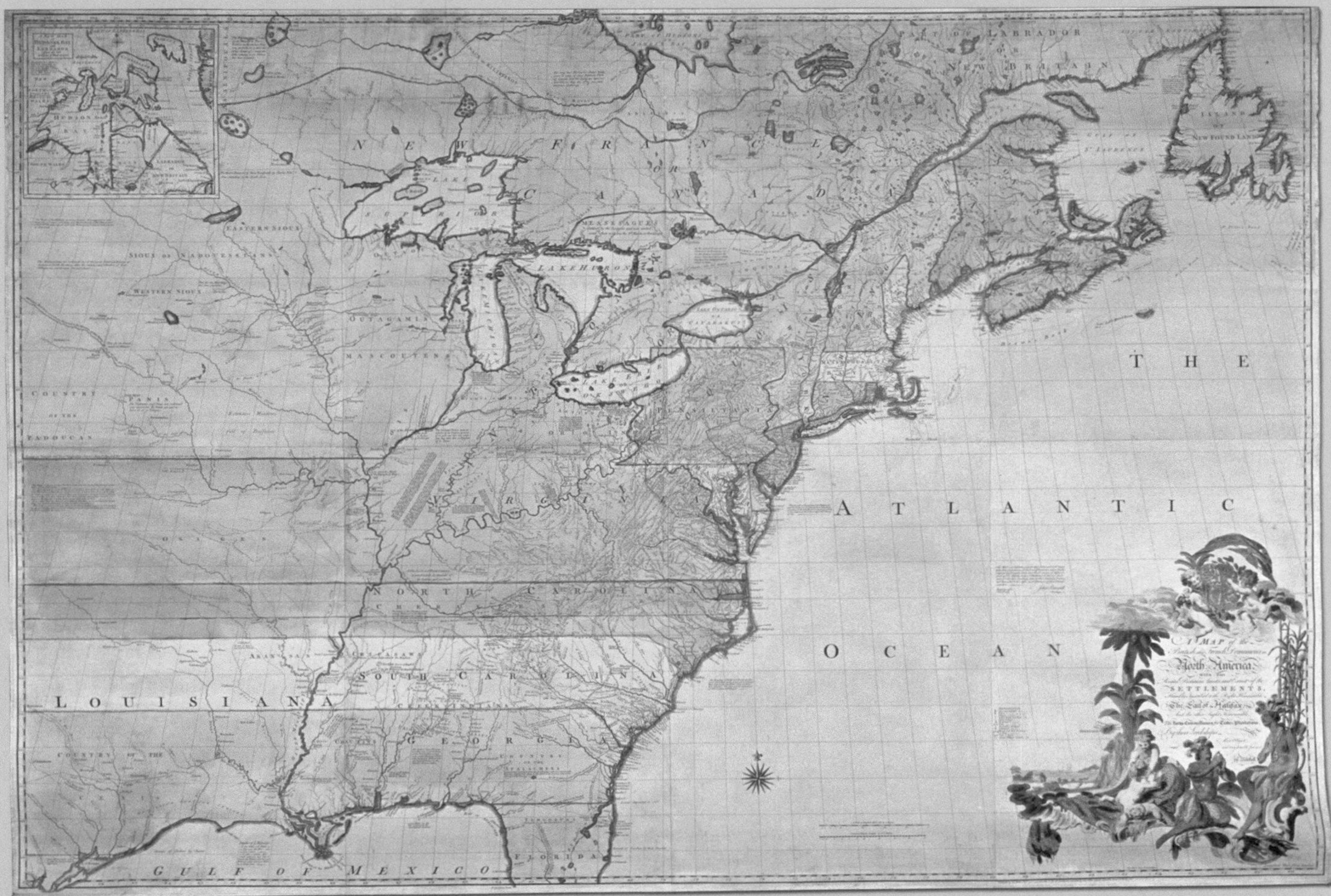

***A Map of the British and French Dominions in North America*, 1755**
John Mitchell (cartographer)
Thomas Kitchen (engraver)
Black and white line engraving with period color, 53-1/4 x 76-5/8 inches
The Colonial Williamsburg Foundation

Trained as a medical doctor, native Virginian John Mitchell developed a deep interest and proficiency in botany. He is best remembered, however, for his 1755 map of the British colonies in North America. In striking contrast to contemporary French cartographers, who depicted the British colonies circumscribed by the Appalachian Mountains, Mitchell presented an expansive view of British North America. The map proved instantly popular in Britain and America, where copies were distributed to each of the colonial governors.

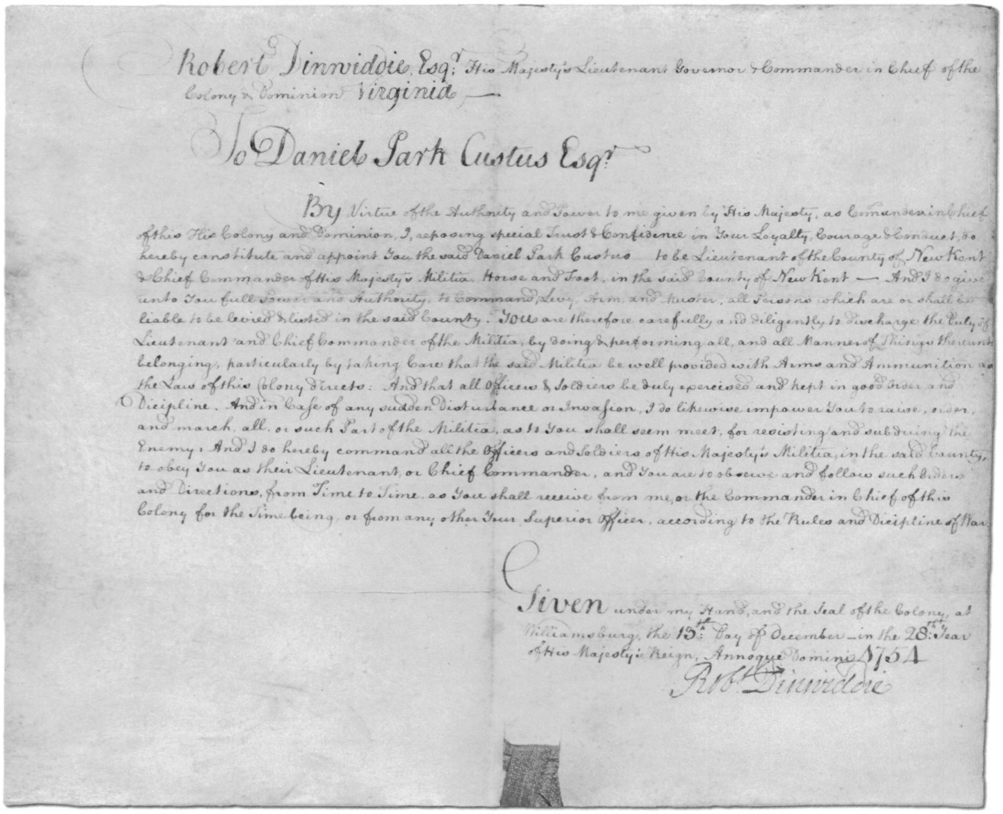

Robert Dinwiddie Esq.r His Majesty's Lieutenant Governor & Commander in Chief of the Colony & Dominion Virginia —

To Daniel Park Custus Esq.r

By Virtue of the Authority and Power to me given by His Majesty, as Commander in Chief of this His Colony and Dominion, I, reposing special Trust & Confidence in Your Loyalty, Courage & Conduct, do hereby constitute and appoint You the said Daniel Park Custus to be Lieutenant of the County of New Kent & Chief Commander of His Majesty's Militia, Horse and Foot, in the said County of New Kent — And I do give unto You full Power and Authority, to Command, Levy, Arm, and Muster, all Persons which are or shall be liable to be levied & listed in the said County. You are therefore carefully and diligently to discharge the Duty of Lieutenant and Chief Commander of the Militia, by doing & performing all, and all Manner of Things thereunto belonging, particularly by taking Care that the said Militia be well provided with Arms and Ammunition as the Law of this Colony directs: And that all Officers & Soldiers be duly exercised and kept in good Order and Discipline. And in Case of any sudden Disturbance or Invasion, I do likewise impower You to raise, order, and march, all, or such Part of the Militia, as to You shall seem meet, for resisting and subduing the Enemy: And I do hereby command all the Officers and Soldiers of His Majesty's Militia, in the said County, to obey You as their Lieutenant, or Chief Commander, and You are to observe and follow such Orders and Directions, from Time to Time, as You shall receive from me, or the Commander in Chief of this Colony for the Time being, or from any other Your Superior Officer, according to the Rules and Discipline of War.

Given under my Hand, and the Seal of the Colony, at Williamsburg, the 13th Day of December in the 28th Year of His Majesty's Reign, Annoque Domini 1754

Rob.t Dinwiddie

Commission: Gov. Robert Dinwiddie appoints Daniel Parke Custis as lieutenant in Virginia militia, 1754
Ink on vellum with wafer seal,
12-1/2 x 15 inches
Special Collections, John D. Rockefeller, Jr. Library, Colonial Williamsburg Foundation, 2002.5

DANIEL PARKE CUSTIS (PARK CUSTUS ON THE DOCUMENT), one of the wealthiest men in Virginia, received this colonel's commission in the Virginia militia from Governor Dinwiddie in December 1754. Custis died suddenly in 1757, and two years later his young widow Martha Dandridge Custis (1731-1802) married George Washington.

THIS EARLY PIPE TOMAHAWK, similar to unmarked examples found on mid-18th-century sites in Western Pennsylvania and Ohio, may have belonged to John Fraser. A Pennsylvania-based Indian trader and gunsmith, Fraser began working in the region in the 1740s. He provided George Washington and guide Christopher Gist shelter during their 1753 trip to deliver a summons to the French commander on the Ohio. Fraser's home at Turtle Creek (east of Pittsburgh) was the site of British General Edward Braddock's 1755 defeat.

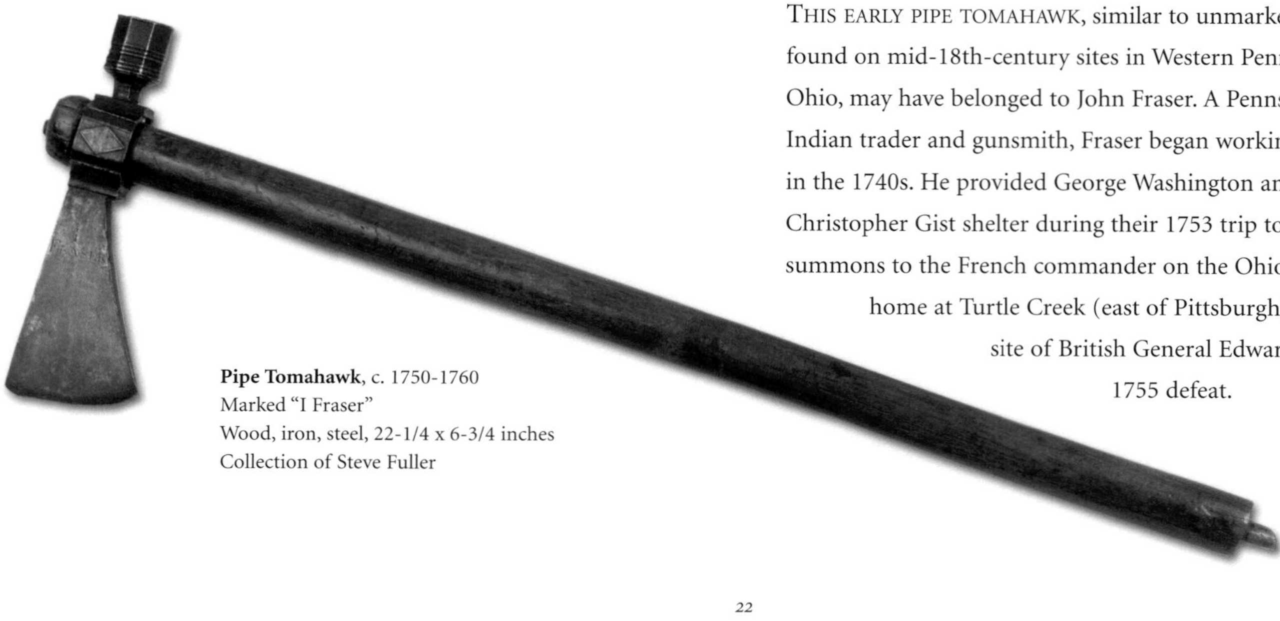

Pipe Tomahawk, c. 1750-1760
Marked "I Fraser"
Wood, iron, steel, 22-1/4 x 6-3/4 inches
Collection of Steve Fuller

Colonel Abraham Barnes, c. 1753-54
John Wollaston
Oil on canvas, 50-1/4 x 40-1/4 inches
Corcoran Gallery of Art, Washington, D.C., Museum Purchase, Gallery Fund and gift of the Honorable Orme Wilson

Native Virginian Abraham Barnes settled in St. Mary's County, Maryland, as a young man and went on to hold a number of important public posts in his adopted colony. A successful merchant, Barnes served as representative in Maryland's Lower House of Assembly from 1745-54. He ranked as major in the colony's militia when he sat for this portrait. His plain scarlet dress, silk sash, sword, and gilt medal gorget — a piece of vestigial armor worn as a symbol of rank — probably approximates George Washington's dress as a major in the militia of neighboring Virginia.

George Washington: Defeat at the Great Meadows, July 3, 1754
Gerry Embleton, 2005
Photograph by Rob Long

Washington's men built a small fort at the natural clearing of Great Meadows, expecting a European-style battle across the open field. Instead, Jumonville's brother attacked on July 3, 1754, by using the cover of the surrounding forest. By evening, with one-third of his force dead or wounded, Washington surrendered. The document, opposite, written entirely in French, accused him of the "assassination" of Ensign Jumonville, an envoy. Washington blamed Dutch Captain Jacob Van Braam's poor translation for his unintended admission. Still, his first command ended with a dark stain on his reputation.

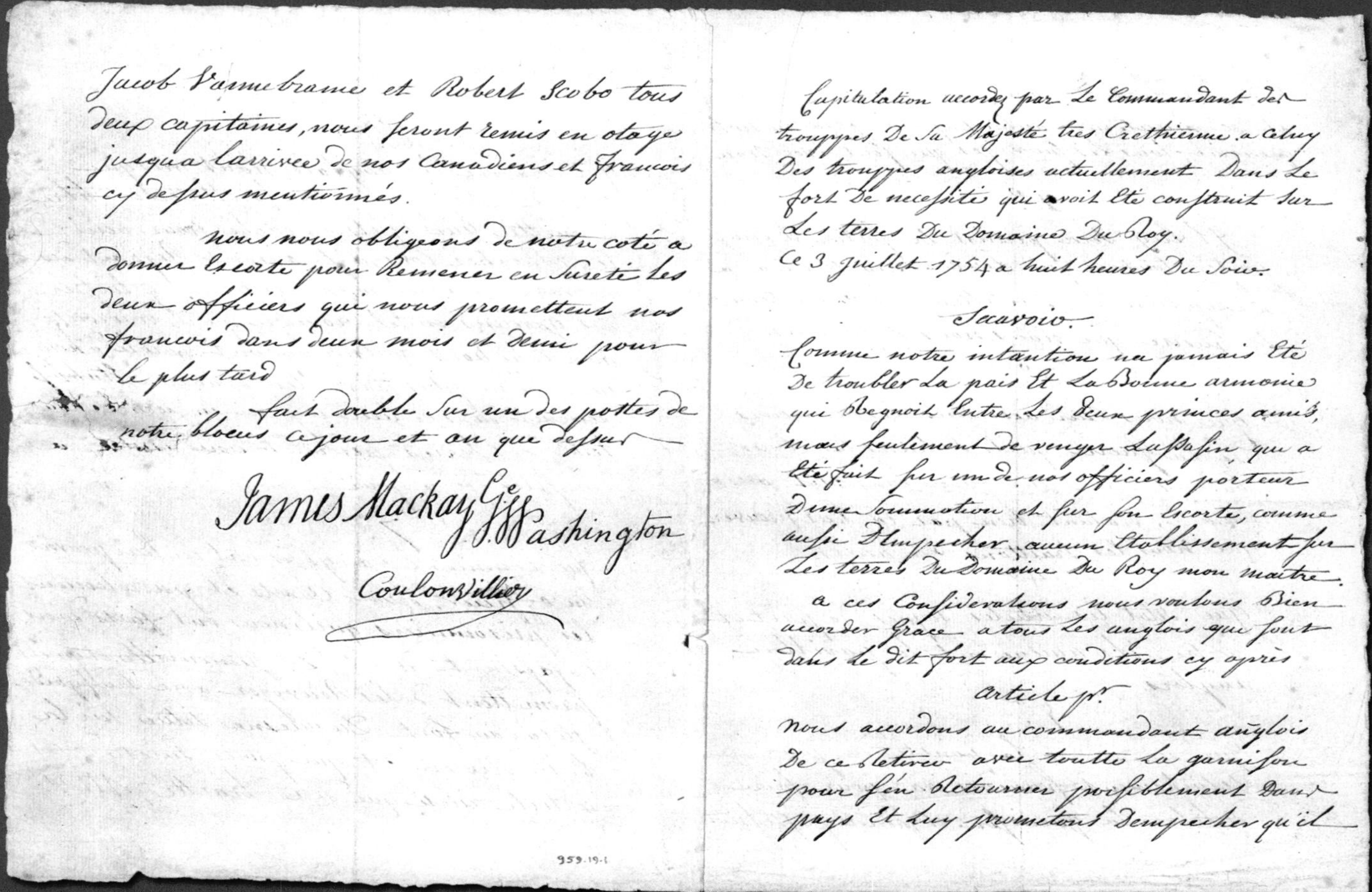
Jacob Vanmebrame et Robert Scobo tous
deux capitaines, nous seront remis en otage
jusqua larrivee de nos Canadiens et François
cy dessus mentionnés.
nous nous obligeons de notre coté a
donner Escorte pour Remener en Sureté les
deux officiers qui nous promettent nos
françois dans deux mois et demi pour
le plus tard
fait double Sur un des postes de
notre blocus a jour et an que dessus
James Mackay Go Washington
Coulonvillier

959.19.1

Capitulation accordé par Le Commandant des
trouppes De Sa Majesté tres Crethienne a celuy
Des trouppes angloises actuellement Dans Le
fort De necessité qui avoit Eté construit Sur
Les terres Du Domaine Du Roy.
Ce 3 juillet 1754 a huit heures Du Soir.
Scavoir.
Comme notre intantion na jamais Eté
De troubler La paix Et La Bonne armonie
qui Regnoit Entre Les deux princes amis,
mais seulement de venger Lassassin qui a
Eté fait sur un de nos officiers porteur
Dune Sommation et sur son Escorte, comme
aussi Dempecher aucun Etablissement sur
Les terres Du Domaine Du Roy mon maitre.
a ces Considerations nous voulons Bien
accorder Grace a tous les anglois qui sont
dans le dit fort aux conditions cy apres
article pr.
nous accordons au commandant anglois
De se Retirer avec toutte la garnison
pour s'en Retourner paisiblement dans son
pays Et luy promettons Dempecher quil

Treaty of Fort Necessity, 3 July 1754
Manuscript, ribbed paper on four pages, 8-1/2 x 11 inches
Last and first pages
On loan from the Royal Ontario Museum, gift of Dr. Sigmund Samuel

AFTER ATTACKING A SMALL PARTY OF FRENCH AND CANADIANS under the command of Ensign Joseph Coulon de Villiers de Jumonville on May 28, 1754, Virginia Lieutenant Colonel George Washington began construction of a small stockade fort at the nearby Great Meadows. Dubbed "Fort Necessity," this post was attacked on July 3, 1754, by a French, Canadian, and Indian force led by Jumonville's brother. Washington and co-commander James Mackay signed this capitulation document after a desperate battle that left one-third of the British forces dead or wounded.

Chapter 4

The Great Warpaths

News of the French and Indian victory at Fort Necessity reached Albany, New York, during a treaty conference between representatives of several northern British colonies and the Iroquois Confederacy. "Brethren," the Mohawk leader Theyanoguin (known as Hendrick) told the colonial delegates, "the Governor of Virginia and the Governor of Canada are both quarrelling about lands which belong to us, and such a quarrel as this may end in our destruction; they fight who shall have the land."

This struggle spread in 1755 to the borderlands between Canada, New York, New England, and Iroquoia. For five years, fighting centered on control of two strategic corridors. A north-south route linked Montreal and New York by Lake Champlain and the Hudson River. An east-west passage ran between Lake Ontario and Albany, following the Mohawk Valley. Tens of thousands of combatants clashed in these campaigns before the surprising conclusion of the conflict in 1760.

British Maneuvers

The long, narrow body of water known as Lake St. Sacrament to Canadians and as Lake George (after 1755) to British colonists flows north from the fringes of the Adirondack Mountains into Lake Champlain. During peacetime, hunters and trappers, traders and smugglers used this route between Canada, Albany, and New England. During the frequent colonial wars, raiding parties and armies, captives and plunder traveled up and down the placid waters.

From their bases at Fort Carillon (Ticonderoga) in the north and Fort William Henry in the south, British, French, and Indian forces struggled desperately for control of this strategic lake. For a few months each year, the camps and garrisons along its shores made the region the most densely populated place in North America.

The British war effort brought together tens of thousands of men (and thousands of women and children) from across the Atlantic World. Only a third of British soldiers in North America were native-born. Two-thirds were Scots and Irish, with the remainder a mixture of Germans, Swiss, and other Europeans (including Hungarians and Norwegians), as well as

American colonists. In some British camps, visitors were as likely to hear Scottish Gaelic or German as English. A few American Indians even carried arms and wore the red coats of the British army.

British Soldiers Had Much to Learn

"You might as well send a Cow in pursuit of a Hare," Virginia provincial officer Adam Stephen observed in 1755, "as an English Soldier loaded in their way with a Coat, Jacket &c. &c. &c. after Canadians in their Shirts, who can shoot and run well, or Naked Indians accustomed to the Woods." A fully loaded British soldier on the march carried at least 63 pounds of clothing, arms, and equipment. But during the American war, British commanders quickly adapted to the challenges of forest campaigning, teaching their soldiers to take cover behind trees like their Canadian, Indian, and American counterparts. Specially raised units of rangers and "light infantry" with lighter clothing, arms, and equipment specialized in skirmishes and irregular warfare.

Two bloody actions have long captured the imagination of historians and novelists, tourists and moviemakers. In August 1757, a force of French, Canadian, and Indian fighters under Louis-Joseph de Montcalm besieged Fort William Henry for three days. When the defeated British and Americans began to march off according to terms negotiated without Montcalm's Indian allies, angry warriors seized prisoners. Some who were sick, wounded, or those who resisted were killed. This incident inspired James Fenimore Cooper's novel *Last of the Mohicans* (1826), perhaps the best-known story about the French and Indian War.

The British returned in 1758 with 16,000 British and American soldiers. On July 8, a force of only 3,600 French soldiers defeated this powerful army at Fort Carillon when the British commander ordered a direct assault on Montcalm's fortified position. The carnage of this day moved Scottish writer Robert Lewis Stevenson to pen the poem "Ticonderoga: A Legend of the West Highlands" (1882).

A French or Canadian Way of War?

The two leaders responsible for defending New France, Canadian Governor General Pierre de Rigaud de Vaudreuil and French commander Marquis de Montcalm, argued passionately about tactics and strategy. Vaudreuil understood that Canada had for generations held out against the British colonies by employing Indian allies and guerilla tactics to attack their settlements.

Canadian militia and the *Troupes de la Marine* excelled in this kind of warfare, which kept their enemies on the defensive and unable to invade New France. To a European professional such as Montcalm, these tactics were uncivilized. Montcalm's French regulars were too few to dismiss his Canadian and Indian allies, but he increasingly settled into a static defense against British assaults. When large British expeditions finally reached the St. Lawrence Valley in 1759-60, Canada capitulated.

***View of the Lines at Lake George*, 1774**
Thomas Davies
Signed "T.D. 1774" in lower left corner
Oil on canvas, 25-1/2 x 30-3/8 inches
Collection of the Fort Ticonderoga Museum

THIS LOVELY LANDSCAPE is the earliest-known painting of the southern end of Lake George, called Lake St. Sacrament by the French. British artillery officer and artist Thomas Davies (c. 1737-1812) accompanied Major General Jeffery Amherst's successful 1759 campaign against the French Forts Carillon (Ticonderoga) and St. Frederic (Crown Point). His work depicts the tent encampment of Amherst's army stretching from the ruins of Fort William Henry in the left rear to the rising ground on the right where William Johnson and Hendrick's provincial and Iroquois forces encamped in 1755.

THEYANOGUIN (1692-1755), or Hendrick as he was known to the British, lived in the Mohawk community of Canajoharie west of Albany, New York. Hendrick traveled to London to meet King George II in 1740, an occasion that may be commemorated in this engraved portrait. In 1755, Hendrick led several hundred Iroquois warriors — mostly Mohawks — in support of a British campaign against the French Fort St. Frederic at Crown Point.

The brave old Hendrick the great sachem or Chief of the Mohawk Indians…, c. 1740
Etching and engraving,
15-1/8 x 10-3/4 inches
Library of Congress, Washington, D.C.

British Shot Pouch, c. 1755
Leather, 7 inches
Collection of Charles Thayer

ON THE MORNING OF SEPTEMBER 8, 1755, Massachusetts provincial soldier Lemuel Lyman was wounded in an ambush known as the "Bloody Morning Scout" when a bullet struck his hand, shattered the stock of his musket, and passed through this leather pouch. Ambushed by a force of French-allied Indians, Canadian militiamen, and elite French grenadiers under the command of French commander Jean-Armand Dieskau, Baron de Dieskau, the provincial and Mohawk force fled to their camp at Lake George. A participant called the ensuing battle "the most awful day that my eyes ever beheld, & may I not say that ever was seen in New England."

Powder Horn, 1756
Attributed to John Bush
Inscribed "Colo Nathan Whiting Esqr / His Horn made at Fort Wm henry / The 11th of Octbr, AD 1756 / when Bows and weighty Spears were us'd in / Fight. Twere nervous Limbs Declrd. A man of might / But Now Gun powder Scorns such strength to Own / And heroes not by Limbs but Souls are Shown / War"
Cow horn, pine, iron, 16 x 3 (plug end) inches
The Connecticut Historical Society Museum, Hartford, Connecticut

POWDER HORNS, LIKE THIS ONE engraved by African-American provincial soldier John Bush, served a practical purpose but also might commemorate the owner's military experiences, places visited, or battles fought.

Wine Cup, 18th century
Engraved with the coat-of-arms of Louis-Joseph Montcalm, Marquis de Montcalm, Marked "I.B.L."
Silver, 6 x 6.5 cm
McCord Museum of Canadian History, Montreal, Gift of David Ross McCord

THIS SILVER WINE CUP, made in France during the early 18th century, was part of French General Montcalm's field equipment during his campaigns in North America. After a series of victories against British and American forces, Montcalm was mortally wounded at the Battle of Quebec, September 13, 1759.

THIS BAYONET WAS USED BY A SOLDIER in the British 50th Regiment, a unit of American recruits from New England and the middle colonies (Pennsylvania, Maryland, Virginia) led by British officers and commanded by Massachusetts Governor William Shirley. It is marked with a regimental, company, and "rack" or individual soldier's number (50th. Rt./f/32), and may have been captured by the French at the siege of Oswego in 1756.

British Bayonet, Early Land Pattern, 1740s (issued 1754)
Engraved "50th Rt./f/32"
Iron with steel point, 21-1/2 x 2-1/2 inches
Private Collection

John Bush: Massachusetts Soldier at Lake George, 1756
Gerry Embleton, 2005
Photograph by Rob Long

"Honorable Sir," an aged George Bush wrote in a September 1758 plea for help to the colonial governor of Massachusetts, "I have a Son In Captivity at Cannaday if he be Living that was Taken Last year at Lake George. . . . His naime is John Bush." George Bush, a free Black farmer and ex-slave from South America, had already lost two sons in the war; now another was missing.

Thirty-year-old John Bush had served in the colony's militia and provincial forces since 1747, spending the winter of 1755-56 at Fort William Henry. He was captured when the fort fell to French and Indian forces in August 1757. Bush died the following year aboard a ship carrying prisoners to France.

Literate and possessing a steady hand, John Bush fashioned exquisitely engraved powder horns on the Lake George frontier in 1755-56. His work inspired other artists to develop a unique style of powder horn engraving that flourished in New England through the end of the American Revolution.

Lieutenant Colonel Nathan Whiting, c. 1768
Attributed to John Durand
Oil on canvas, 43 x 31 inches
The Connecticut Historical Society Museum,
Hartford, Connecticut

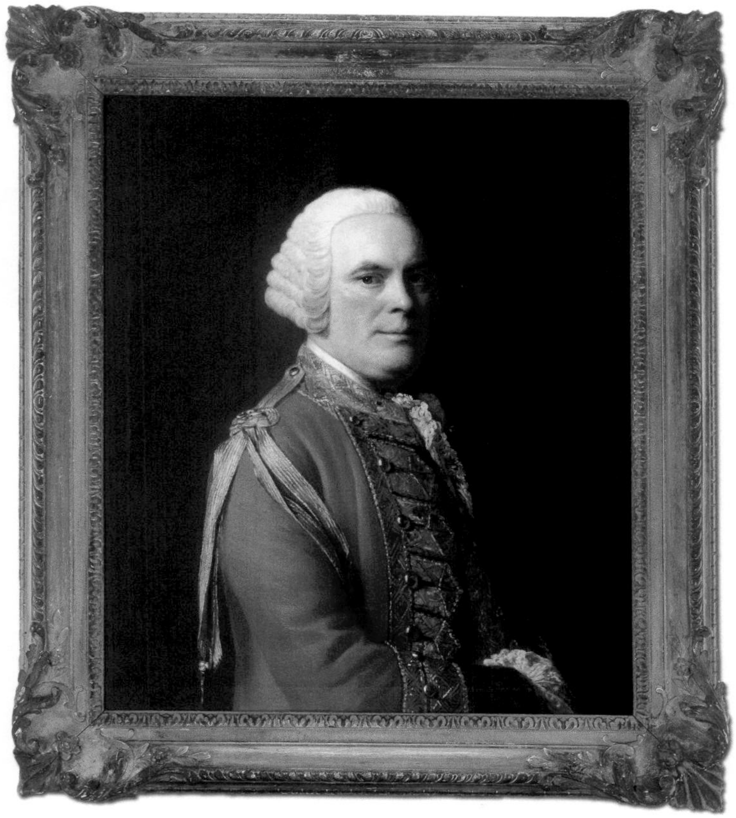

Lieutenant General James Abercromby, c. 1760
Allan Ramsay
Oil on canvas, 30-1/2 x 25-1/2 inches
Collection of the Fort Ticonderoga Museum

LIKE MANY NEW ENGLAND OFFICERS in the French and Indian War, Connecticut native Nathan Whiting (1724-1771) served as a young man on the expedition that captured the French fortress Louisburg on Cape Breton Island in 1745. Whiting returned to service in 1755, taking command of a Connecticut regiment on the expedition against Fort St. Frederic. Present at the Bloody Morning Scout, he skillfully organized a fighting retreat to the provincial camp. Promoted to Colonel in 1756, he served through the end of the war, and was given a British commission before being reduced to half-pay when peace came in 1763.

MAJOR GENERAL JAMES ABERCROMBY (1706-1781), one of many Scottish officers in the British army, arrived in North America in 1756 as deputy to British Commander-in-Chief John Campbell, Earl of Loudoun. As Loudoun's successor in 1758, Abercromby led a force of more than 16,000 British and American troops against the French Fort Carillon, known to the British as Ticonderoga. In a surprise defeat that was as stunning to the outnumbered defenders (four to one) as it was to Abercromby's army, the Anglo-American force suffered horrendous casualties while assaulting a fortified position protected by French regulars led by Louis-Joseph, Marquis de Montcalm. This portrait was painted after Abercromby was recalled to Britain at the end of 1758, and passed down through his descendents as part of a group of family portraits.

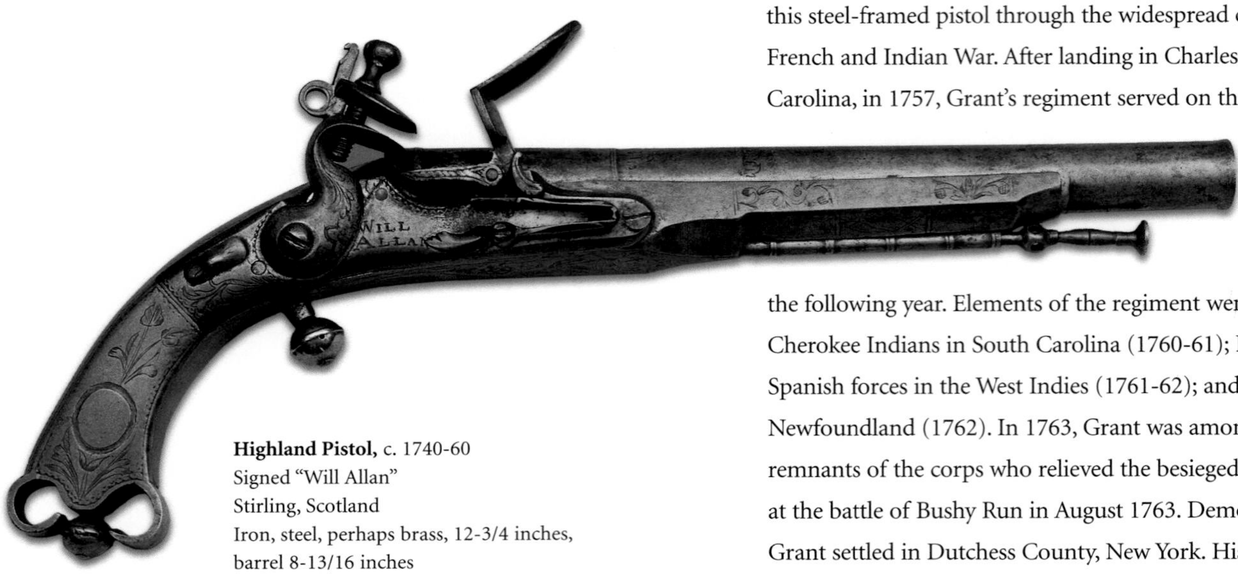

Highland Pistol, c. 1740-60
Signed "Will Allan"
Stirling, Scotland
Iron, steel, perhaps brass, 12-3/4 inches,
barrel 8-13/16 inches
Private Collection

Along with his basket-hilted backsword, James Grant carried this steel-framed pistol through the widespread campaigns of the French and Indian War. After landing in Charleston, South Carolina, in 1757, Grant's regiment served on the 1758 expedition against Fort Duquesne, and on the Lake George frontier the following year. Elements of the regiment went on to battle Cherokee Indians in South Carolina (1760-61); French and Spanish forces in the West Indies (1761-62); and French forces in Newfoundland (1762). In 1763, Grant was among the sickly remnants of the corps who relieved the besieged Fort Pitt, fighting at the battle of Bushy Run in August 1763. Demobilized in 1764, Grant settled in Dutchess County, New York. His descendents carefully preserved his sword, pistol, and military papers for more than 200 years.

The British government met the demands of the Seven Years' War by recruiting thousands of non-English-speaking Protestants into the army. In addition to German-speaking recruits from Europe and the American colonies, the British recruited heavily in the Scottish Highlands, an economically depressed region from which soldiers had long been an export. One inducement for enlisting in the Highland battalions was the opportunity to wear traditional dress and arms, including tartan kilts and basket-hilted swords that had been banned by the British government following the Jacobite uprising of 1745-46. Ensign James Grant of the First Highland Battalion (62nd, later 77th Regiment), a native of Kinmachlie, Banffshire, Scotland, carried this sword in the French and Indian War.

Highland Officer's Backsword,
c. 1740-60
Stirling, Scotland
Steel, iron, 37 inches,
blade 31-5/8 inches
Private Collection

General Johnson Saving a Wounded French Officer from the Tomahawk of a North American Indian, c. 1764-68
Benjamin West,
Oil on Canvas, 129.5 x 106.5 cm
Derby Museums and Art Gallery, UK

THIS PAINTING, ONE OF PENNSYLVANIA-BORN ARTIST Benjamin West's (1738-1820) earliest historical works, is believed to commemorate an incident during the 1759 British siege of the French Fort Niagara. On July 24, 1759, British, provincial, and Iroquois fighters intercepted a relief force attempting to reinforce the besieged French garrison. Recent cleaning for the *Clash of Empires* exhibition has revealed a fallen French soldier among the trees on the far left, his four jacket buttons and upside down head visible near the tree roots.

Chapter 5

The Backcountry War

"Virginia is a Country Young at War," George Washington observed two-and-a-half years after his defeat at Fort Necessity. "Until the breaking out of these disturbances [it] has lived in the most profound and Tranquil peace; never studying war nor warfare." Washington's comments characterize as well the neighboring colonies of Maryland and Pennsylvania, which began the 1750s with weak or no militias and few forts or public stores of arms.

After a 1755 British expedition failed to capture Fort Duquesne, French, Canadian, and Indian fighters launched devastating raids against the Pennsylvania, Maryland, and Virginia backcountries. Similar attacks had long protected New France and Indian nations. The British would not retake the Forks of the Ohio until 1758, when they finally persuaded the Ohio Indians that their homelands would be protected from encroachment only if they would ally against the French.

March to the Monongahela

Hoping to counter French encroachments without starting a general war, British officials decided to send more regular troops and a British commander to North America in 1755. Sixty-year-old Major General Edward Braddock personally led the expedition against Fort Duquesne. George Washington, who had resigned from the Virginia Regiment over a dispute concerning his rank, joined the campaign as one of Braddock's aides.

French commander Captain Claude-Pierre Pecaudy de Contrecoeur knew that Fort Duquesne's wood and earth walls could not withstand a siege by Braddock's formidable artillery and 1,400 soldiers. His only hope lay in a preemptive attack on the British before they reached the Forks of the Ohio. On July 9, 1755, a force of 637 Indian warriors joined 250 French and Canadian fighters to gain a stunning victory along the Monongahela River.

"I have often heard the British officers call the Indians undisciplined savages," Pennsylvanian James Smith remarked after five years' captivity among the Ohio Indians, "which is a capital mistake." Smith observed, "They are under good command, and are punctual in obeying orders; they can act in concert, and when their officers lay a plan and give orders, they will cheerfully unite."

Many Europeans considered native war practices cruel and uncivilized, and few understood the cultural meanings behind them. The widespread tradition of "mourning war" helps explain these customs. Faced with devastating losses from disease and conflict, many families and communities eased their grief for lost kin by adopting war captives into their nations. "They rarely kill those who can be taken prisoner," a veteran French officer observed of the Iroquois, "because the honor and advantage of victory lie in bringing prisoners back to the village." Nonetheless, the scalp or ritual torture of a captive sometimes took the place of adoption.

Defending the Backcountry

Pennsylvania, Maryland, and Virginia were unprepared when, with French support, Delaware, Shawnee, and other warriors attacked unprotected frontier settlements after Braddock's defeat. Swift raids by war parties with as few as a dozen fighters created thousands of refugees, stretching from the Delaware Water Gap in eastern Pennsylvania to the Carolina backcountry. More than 1,000 inhabitants were carried into captivity; perhaps 1,500 more lost their lives in the attacks.

To counter this threat, the provinces raised regiments of soldiers and erected a line of forts and blockhouses along the eastern edge of the Allegheny Mountains. This stationary defense proved ineffective against the raiders, though it provided valuable military experience to men like George Washington.

Three years after Braddock's defeat, British Brigadier General John Forbes gathered an army "collected from all parts of the globe," including a regiment of Scottish Highlanders, German-speaking redcoats, and Cherokee warriors from the southern Appalachian Mountains.

Forbes understood better than most British commanders that the key to defeating the outnumbered and poorly supplied French was to lure away their allies. He joined provincial and royal officials in pledging that the Ohio Indians' lands would be protected from colonial expansion if they withdrew support for the French. This was a welcome message to peoples weary of war and eager to be free of French and British occupation.

Forbes' army of nearly 5,000 men marched the final 50 miles to the Forks of the Ohio in November 1758. With only a few hundred French and Canadian defenders on hand, the French commander of Fort Duquesne destroyed the fort and withdrew. Forbes claimed the ruins and renamed them Pittsburgh after British Prime Minister William Pitt.

***Captain Robert Orme*, 1756**
Sir Joshua Reynolds
Oil on canvas, 239 x 147 cm
National Portrait Gallery, London

CAPTAIN ROBERT ORME (1732-1790) ACCOMPANIED BRITISH MAJOR GENERAL EDWARD BRADDOCK to Virginia in 1755 as an aide-de-camp for the expedition against the French Fort Duquesne. He developed a close friendship with George Washington, who also served as an aide to Braddock. Wounded at the July 9, 1755, Battle of the Monongahela, Orme returned to Britain, where he posed for this portrait commemorating his American service.

Stove Plate, 1756
Right sideplate of a jamb stove
Inscribed with "DIS IST DAS JAHR DA RIN WITET"
Cast iron, 26-1/2 x 28 inches
Collection of the Moravian Historical Society, Nazareth, Pa.

EIGHTEENTH-CENTURY GERMAN IMMIGRANTS TO PENNSYLVANIA continued an old Central European custom of heating their homes with iron or tile "jamb" stoves that frequently displayed biblical verses and other decoration. This cast iron plate bears the date 1756 and a rare reference to worldly events. The inscription, "This is the year in which rages," continues on an end plate (located at the Mercer Museum, Doylestown, Pa.): DER INCHIN SCHAR ("the Indian War Party"). Ironmasters and customers in Pennsylvania had good reason to remember the year of devastating frontier raids by Delaware, Shawnee, and other warriors from the Ohio Country.

An Indian War chief completely equipped with a scalp in his hand, c. 1751-1758
George Townshend
Pen, ink, and watercolor on paper, 9-1/2 x 6-7/8 inches
National Portrait Gallery, London

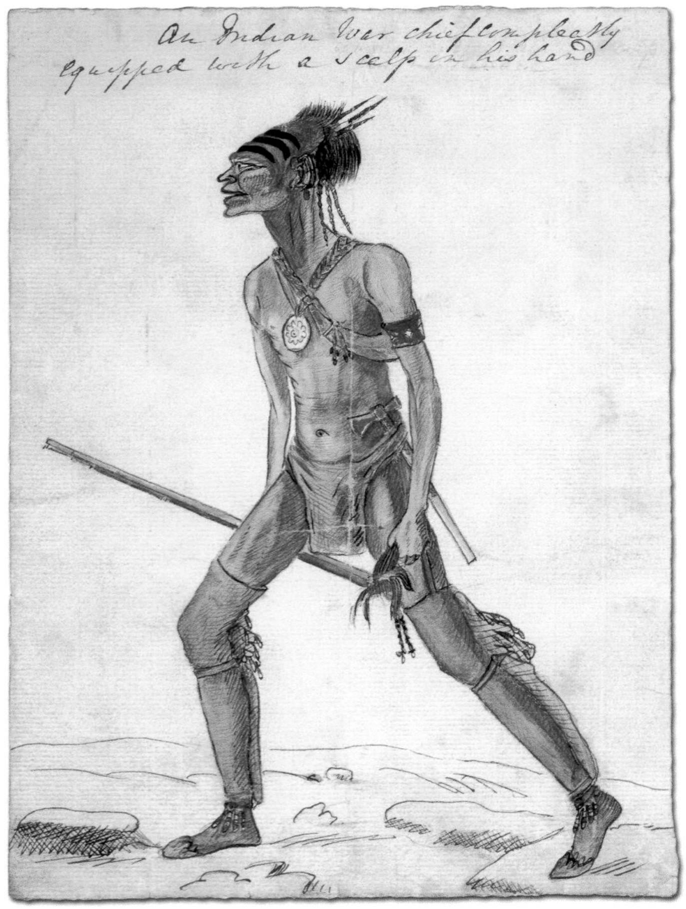

THIS SKETCH CAPTURES THE LIGHT DRESS AND EQUIPMENT favored by Native American warriors on military campaigns. British officer and cartoonist George Townshend (1724-1807) served as a brigadier under General James Wolfe during the 1759 expedition against Quebec.

Martin Lucorney: A Hungarian Red Coat at Braddock's Defeat, July 9, 1755
Gerry Embleton, 2005
Photograph by Rob Long

Private Martin Lucorney of the British Independent Company of New York was near the rear of Braddock's column when shots rang out far ahead. As the firing increased, Hungarian-born Lucorney could hear the fearful sound of Indian warriors' shouts up ahead. Virginia Captain Adam Stephen, stationed nearby, later wrote that the Indians and Canadians "kept on their Bellies in the Bushes and behind the Trees, and took particular Aim at Our Men, and Officers especially." Most of the British troops stood helplessly in ranks or huddled together in the open, easy targets for the deadly fire. A comrade later wrote that Martin, who spoke little English, acted bravely that afternoon, "watching his opportunity to fire upon the enemy" from behind a tree. When asked why he wept toward the end of the battle, Lucorney replied, "it was from Grief for seeing the English retreating." In a final act of heroism, he helped carry the mortally wounded General Braddock from the field.

Scarouyady, 2002
Robert Connell
Oil on canvas, 30 x 24 inches
Courtesy of the artist

As early as the 1740s, Oneida Chief Scarouyady (d. 1758), sometimes called Monacatootha, acted with Seneca chief Tanaghrisson (Half King) as a representative of the Iroquois Confederacy among the Delaware, Shawnee, and other native peoples living near the Forks of the Ohio River. Scarouyady was one of a handful of Indians who accompanied the Braddock expedition against Fort Duquesne in 1755. His son was killed in a friendly fire incident with British soldiers several days before the Battle of the Monongahela. This modern portrait by Pittsburgh artist Robert Connell draws on Captain Robert Orme's 1755 notes and sketch of Scarouyady's distinctive tattoos and war marks.

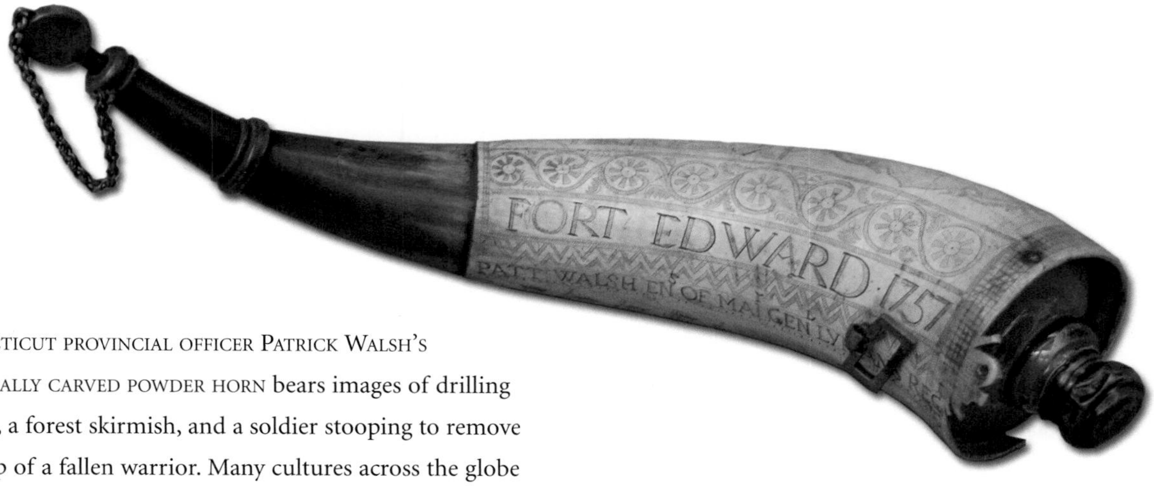

CONNECTICUT PROVINCIAL OFFICER PATRICK WALSH'S ARTISTICALLY CARVED POWDER HORN bears images of drilling soldiers, a forest skirmish, and a soldier stooping to remove the scalp of a fallen warrior. Many cultures across the globe practiced forms of ritualistic mutilation. There is considerable evidence scalping had ancient roots in North America. Colonial Europeans regularly offered bounties for enemy scalps, and some soldiers scalped fallen American Indians.

Powder Horn, 1757
Marked "FORT EDWARD 1757" and "PATT WALSH ENs OF MAJr GENL LYMANS REGT"
Cow horn, glass, silver, brass, and iron, 13 x 3 inches
Huntington Museum of Art, Huntington, West Virginia, bequest of Herman P. Dean

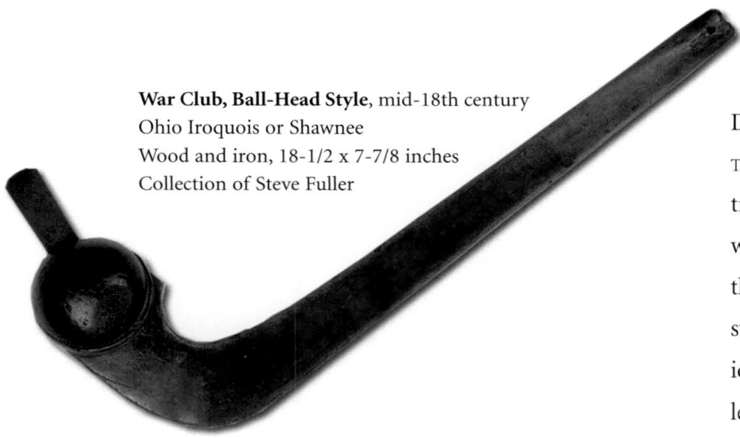

War Club, Ball-Head Style, mid-18th century
Ohio Iroquois or Shawnee
Wood and iron, 18-1/2 x 7-7/8 inches
Collection of Steve Fuller

DESPITE THE WIDESPREAD AVAILABILITY OF TRADE AXES AND PIPE TOMAHAWKS, many Native American warriors continued to use traditional wooden hand weapons, sometimes enhancing them with iron or steel cutting blades. These two examples represent the principal forms used in eastern North America. Iconographic symbols on these and other examples recorded the owner's identity and/or personal war record. Such weapons were often left at the scene of a fight as a "calling card."

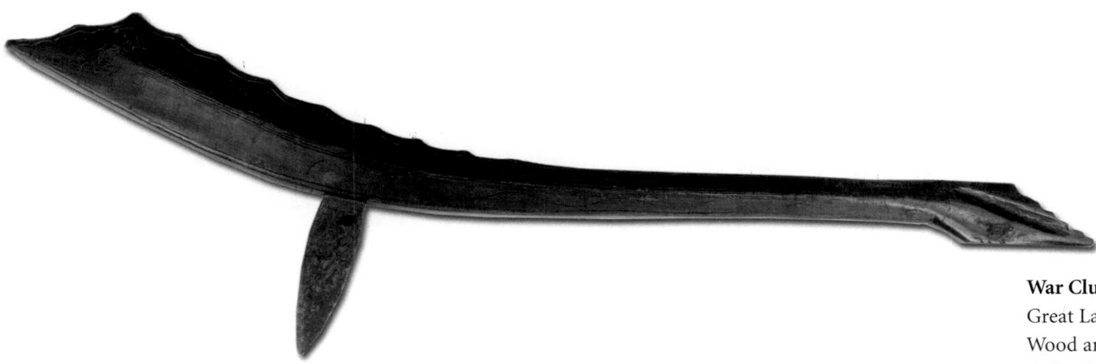

War Club, Sword-Style, c. 18th century
Great Lakes
Wood and iron, 28-1/4 x 6-1/2 inches
Collection of Jim and Carolyn Dresslar

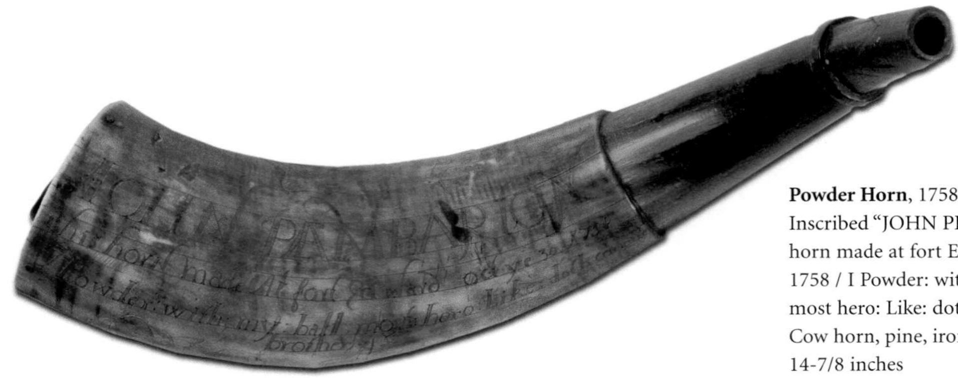

Powder Horn, 1758
Inscribed "JOHN PEMBARTON / his horn made at fort Edward Oct ye 30 1758 / I Powder: with: my: brother ball: most hero: Like: doth concure: all"
Cow horn, pine, iron, and lead, 14-7/8 inches
Collection of William H. Myers

THIS ENGRAVED POWDER HORN bears marks commemorating the military service of two different owners: an Anglo-American soldier and an Indian warrior. Characteristic war marks used by Iroquois and other nations to illustrate personal campaign histories appear on the horn as well as the first owner's name and place of service. The pictographic images include a turtle, probably the symbol by which the warrior was known, as well as rectangular marks representing the number of times he had been to war, and figures representing captives or scalps taken.

THE SITTER HAS BEEN TRADITIONALLY IDENTIFIED as Colonel Edward Fell of Baltimore, Maryland. His uniform matches those worn by the Virginia Regiment (1755-62) and several other American provincial corps. Militia officer Edward Fell is not known to have held a provincial commission, but an Ensign Robert Fell served briefly in the Virginia Regiment in 1757.

Friendly Association Gorget, c. 1757-58
Joseph Richardson
Silver, 5-5/8 x 5 inches
Atwater Kent Museum of Philadelphia, Historical Society of Pennsylvania Collection

PENNSYLVANIA QUAKERS WHO BELIEVED THAT THE BACKCOUNTRY WAR had been caused by cheating the Indians out of their lands formed the Friendly Association for Regaining and Preserving Peace with the Indians by Pacific Measures in 1756. The Association supported diplomatic efforts to end the conflict and purchased presents for distribution at several major councils. Philadelphia silversmith Joseph Richardson engraved this gorget with an image of a colonial figure passing the pipe of peace to an Indian, a motif also used on a silver peace medal struck by the Association in 1757.

Colonel Edward Fell (1737-1766), c. 1764
Attributed to John Hesselius
Oil on canvas, 45-3/4 x 35-19/32 inches
The Maryland Historical Society, Baltimore Maryland, 1986-105-5

Kittanning Medal, 1756
Inscribed: "Kittanning destroyed by Col.^{L} Armstrong" "SEPTEMBER 5 1756"
Silver, 1-3/4 inches diameter
Collection of City of Fredericksburg, loan facilitated by APVA Preservation Virginia and the Hugh Mercer Apothecary Shop

On September 8, 1756, Pennsylvania provincial soldiers attacked and destroyed the Delaware Indian town of Kittanning, located 40 miles north of Fort Duquesne on the Allegheny River. The Corporation of the City of Philadelphia presented each officer with a silver medal commemorating the action: the first American military decoration. This medal descended in the family of Captain Hugh Mercer (1726-1777), a Scottish immigrant who was wounded while leading men in the attack on Kittanning. Mercer served through the French and Indian War and commanded the British post at Pittsburgh after the 1758 Forbes expedition. He practiced medicine in Fredericksburg, Virginia after the war, and as an American brigadier general fell mortally wounded in the January 1777 Battle of Princeton.

Medal to Genl ' Mercer__, by the City of Philad^{a}—

This highly valued medal, in memory of my venerated father, was presented to him by the corporation of the City of Philadelphia, for his bravery and good conduct- as Capt of Infantry in the destruction of Kittanning an Indian Settlement, in the Colony of Pennsylvania, under Colo Armstrong in Sepr 1756, soon after my father came from Scotland in early life

We were then British Colonies, and those Campaigns (commonly called Braddocks war in 1755-'56, when Washington too commenced his military career) were between the colony of Penn^{a} – & the French & Indians- Kittanning was near Pittsburg, now one of the most flourishing cities in the U. States- The French had a fort there, called Du Quesne afterwards Fort Pitt.

Jun^{y} 1835 H. Mercer

An 1835 letter from Mercer's son accompanied the medal, establishing its provenance and recording the family's appreciation of its deep historical significance.

Chapter 6

The Fight for Canada

From 1755 to 1760, British, French, and American Indians engaged in some of the largest and most dramatic military operations of the American war. Campaigns in Atlantic Canada and the St. Lawrence Valley involved joint operations between naval and land forces, as well as large-scale, European-style sieges employing heavy artillery and complex engineering earthworks. The contrast between these operations and the campaigns in the American interior reveal both the remarkable military power that 18th-century empires could project far from Europe and also the limits of that power. The dominance of regular European troops and fleets in these campaigns reinforced the contempt shared by most Europeans toward native and colonial fighters. This perspective shaped profoundly the fate of Britain's American empire after the fall of Canada.

Defending New France

French settlement in Acadia (now western Nova Scotia, eastern New Brunswick, and northeastern Maine) began in the early 1600s. France ceded Acadian territory to the British in 1713, but by 1750, more than 13,000 French-speaking inhabitants were living along the region's extensive coastline. The boundaries were still in dispute when conflict broke out in the Ohio Country in 1754. Most Acadians living in British territory had remained neutral during previous conflicts, but in 1755, fear of insurgency and desire for the Acadians' lands and fishing grounds led New England and British forces to ruthlessly expel the inhabitants. This ethnic displacement scattered Acadians across the British colonies and the larger Atlantic world. Those who settled in Louisiana came to be known as "Cajuns," from the word "Acadian."

Founded in 1719 as a counterweight to British Nova Scotia, the fortress and naval base of Louisburg on Isle Royale (Cape Breton Island) quickly grew into one of the busiest ports in North America. Louisburg's harbor protected French fleets guarding the rich fishing grounds as well as the sea approach to Canada. In 1745, an army of New Englanders and the Royal Navy besieged and took the port. Louisburg was subsequently returned to France by the peace treaty of 1748. During the 1750s, British forces based in Halifax (founded in 1749) were dispatched to fight against French, Canadian, and Acadian fighters as well as Mi'kmaq, Abenaki, and other warriors who opposed British colonial expansion. French ships based at Louisburg continued to provide credible defense for Canada until the successful British siege of 1758.

Founded by Samuel de Champlain in 1608, Quebec, the capital of New France, was blessed with natural defenses in the form of high cliffs and a difficult water approach from the Atlantic Ocean. By 1750, it housed grand public buildings and more than 5,000 inhabitants. British commander James Wolfe arrived in June 1759 with a fleet of 141 vessels, almost 10,000 soldiers, and 13,000 sailors. French commander Montcalm had fewer than 4,000 French regulars, 12,000 militia and *Troupes de la Marine*, and perhaps 1,800 warriors from the Great Lakes and Canada to defend the city and many miles of countryside. After months of ineffective probing attacks and a terror campaign that destroyed 1,400 Canadian farms, Wolfe unexpectedly landed a force west of the city. On September 13, 1759, British troops prevailed in a battle that left both Wolfe and Montcalm dead.

By 1760, France's early success against Britain and her allies was only a distant memory. Denied reinforcements or significant supplies since 1757, French and Canadian forces could only attempt to hold territory with the hope that peace would soon come. Native peoples who had allied themselves with the French suffered from the loss of supplies as well. Support from the Ohio nations, then other Indians, steadily eroded, further weakening New France. Iroquois communities in Canada and the heartland of the Confederacy remained divided through 1759, when many leaders concluded it was wise to forge good relations with the likely winners. More than 800 warriors accompanied one of the three British armies converging on Montreal in September 1760. The city capitulated to Major General Jeffery Amherst five years to the day after the Battle of Lake George/St. Sacrament.

THIS GOLD AND ENAMEL CROSS is the symbol of the Order of Saint-Louis, founded by Louis XV in 1693 to recognize the merit of French Catholic officers with at least 10 years' military service. Many officers of the *Compagnies Franches de la Marine*, including almost 150 Canadians, were awarded the cross and the title *Chevalier de l'Ordre de Saint-Louis* in recognition of their distinguished service in the colonial conflicts in North America. A French officer who served in Canada in the 1750s observed that "those who had been awarded the Cross of Saint-Louis were as highly esteemed as lieutenant generals."

Medal, Order of Saint-Louis, c. 1775-1825
Artist unknown
Front: "LUD. M INST 1693"
Back: "VIRTUTIS PRÆM BELL"
Gold, white enamel, silk ribbon, 13 x 3.4 cm
McCord Museum of Canadian History, Montreal
(M966.22)

Marquis de Boishébert (1727-1797), c. 1753
Artist unknown
Oil on canvas, 81.7 x 65.5 cm
McCord Museum of Canadian History,
Montreal, purchase from Madame Roch Rolland

CHARLES DESCHAMPS DE BOISHÉBERT ENTERED THE *TROUPES DE LA MARINE* AS A CADET IN 1739 and served on the New York frontier, and in Acadia during the 1740s. In 1753, he led the advance detachment of Governor Duquense's fort-building expedition in the Ohio Valley, and from 1755-1758, organized effective partisan resistance to British forces during the expulsion of the Acadians and the siege of Louisburg. In 1759, he led a corps of Acadian volunteers in the defense of Quebec, settling in France after the fall of Canada.

DOMINIC SERRES (1719-1793) EMERGED AS THE DOMINANT BRITISH MARITIME PAINTER during the Seven Years' War. Born in France, he was captured at sea during the War of the Austrian Succession (1741-48) and settled in London after his imprisonment. Rising British patriotism and interest in the string of worldwide victories that began in 1758 generated a rich market for epic paintings, prints, and other commemorative pieces. One of the first products to reach the market was a set of 12 prints chronicling the British campaign against Quebec in 1759. British naval officer Richard Short, a talented draughtsman, provided on-the-spot sketches. These four oil paintings, signed and dated by Serres in 1760, are believed to be worked up from Short's drawings to serve as models for the engravers.

THE CATHOLIC BISHOP OF QUEBEC OVERSAW RELIGIOUS AFFAIRS in New France. The view below chronicles heavy damage to Quebec's Lower Town caused by the British bombardment during the siege of 1759.

***The Bishop's House with the Ruined Town of Quebec the St. Lawrence Beyond*, 1760**
Dominic Serres
Oil on canvas, 33.6 x 52 cm
The Beaverbrook Art Gallery, purchased with funds from a Minister of Communications Cultural Property Grant and the General Purchase Fund, 1992.02

***The Intendant's Palace, Quebec*, 1760**
Dominic Serres
Oil on canvas, 33.6 x 52 cm
The Beaverbrook Art Gallery, purchased with funds from a Minister of Communications Cultural Property Grant and the General Purchase Fund, 1992.01

THE CIVIL OFFICIAL KNOWN AS THE INTENDANT oversaw economic affairs and the administration of justice in New France.

A View of the Church of Notre-Dame-de-la-Victoire, Quebec City, Quebec, 1760
Dominic Serres
Oil on canvas, 35.2 x 50.2 cm
Bibliothéque et Archives Canada/Library and Archives Canada/C-025662

This church in Quebec's Lower Town was named *Notre-Dame-de-la-Victoire* (Blessed Mother of the Victory) in 1690 following the retreat of British Admiral Phipps' expedition against the city. Gutted by fire and British bombardment in 1759, it was later restored and remains the centerpiece of the city's Palace Royale.

A View of the Treasury and Jesuits College, Quebec City, Quebec, 1760
Dominic Serres
Oil on canvas, 35.5 x 50.5 cm
Bibliothéque et Archives Canada/Library and Archives Canada/C-025663

In this view based on Richard Short's eyewitness drawings, Canadian families and British sailors survey the destruction following the siege of Quebec.

THIS GOLD MEDAL IS AN EARLY EXAMPLE OF THE ORDER worn by members of The Loyal and Friendly Society of the Blew and Orange, a fraternal Protestant organization founded by members of the British 4th Regiment of Foot around 1730. Members of the order in other British regiments served in North America during the French and Indian War.

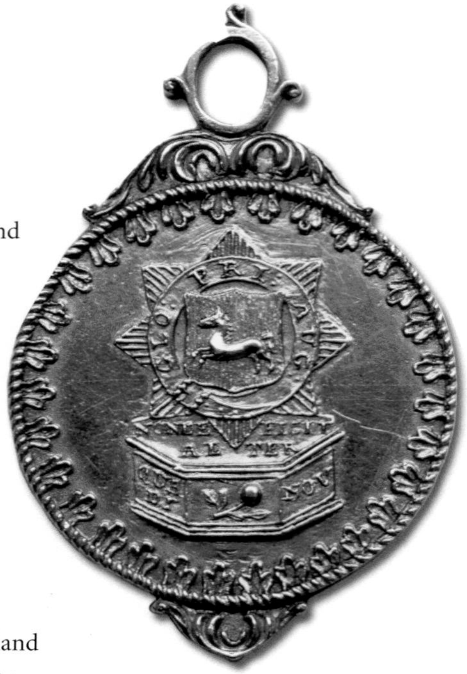

The Loyal and Friendly Society of the Blew and Orange Medal, c. 1727-60
Cast and chased gold,
1-3/4 x 1-1/4 inches
Private Collection

JAMES THOMPSON OF TAIN, Scotland, entered the Second Highland Battalion (63rd, later 78th Regiment) as a sergeant in 1757. This Scottish regiment served in the campaigns against Louisburg (1758) and Quebec (1759), and remained in Canada after the fall of Montreal in 1760. When the corps was disbanded in 1763, many demobilized officers and men, including Sergeant Thompson, took advantage of generous land grants and remained in North America. Thompson acquired these long bladed daggers, known as dirks, during the French and Indian War.

Dirk, date unknown
Artist unknown
Inscribed "Ja. Tompson"
Wood, metal, skin,
4.5 x 43 x 4.3 cm
Canadian War
Museum Collection

Dirk, date unknown
Artist unknown
Inscribed with masonic symbol
Wood, metal, skin,
3.3 x 35.3 x 3.2 cm
Canadian War
Museum Collection

Sir Jeffery Amherst (1717-1797), 1765
Joshua Reynolds
Oil on canvas, 50 x 40 inches
Mead Art Museum, Amherst College, Amherst, Massachusetts, Museum Purchase, AC 1967.85

After Jeffrey Amherst returned to Britain in 1764, British artist Joshua Reynolds produced this dramatic portrait of the commander. It portrays Amherst as the conqueror of Canada, a map of Montreal lying under an iron helmet before him. In the background, British troops descend the rapids of the St. Lawrence River, a feat facilitated by Iroquois guides who accompanied the 1760 expedition.

Troopboat, c. 1758
Artist unknown
Wood, cork, brass, silver, paint,
117 x 490 x 360 mm
National Maritime Museum,
London, Greenwich Hospital
Collection, SLR0499

In spite of traditional hostility between the land and sea services, the British army and navy made great strides during the Seven Years' War in developing tools and tactics for combined operations. This is an original model of a shallow draft troop boat developed in 1758 for amphibious landings by British troops. Experience gained during campaigns against Louisburg (1758) and Quebec (1759) contributed to a series of stunning combined operations in the Carribbean, culminating in the June 7, 1762, landing of 11,800 redcoats near Havana, Cuba, with no fatalities.

After the fall of Canada in 1760, British Commander-in-Chief Jeffrey Amherst commissioned 182 silver medals for presentation to the warriors who had remained with his army during the campaign against Montreal. The medals bear an image of the city of Montreal, with the nation and name of the warrior to whom they were presented engraved on the back; in this case, a Mohican named "Tankalkel." Amherst presented a gold example (location unknown) to Superintendent of Indian Affairs William Johnson.

Medal, c. 1760
Daniel Christian Fueter
Perhaps silver, 45 cm diameter
Bibliothéque et Archives
Canada/Library and Archives Canada

Pouch, 18th century
artist unknown
Hide, quill, brass, hair,
68 x 31 x 3 cm
The Field Museum, gift of
Mrs. A. W. F. Fuller 1964
(2820.155563)

This leather pouch, decorated with dyed porcupine quills, sheet metal cones, and red deer hair, is believed to have been collected in North America during the French and Indian War. It was then passed down through generations of the Amherst family. Amherst's 1763 policies toward Native Americans after the fall of Canada sparked a widespread uprising against British forces in the Great Lakes and Ohio Country.

Honor in Defeat: An Officer of the Royal-Roussillon Regiment at Montreal, September 7, 1760
Gerry Embleton, 2005
Photograph by Rob Long

In retaliation for what he considered French collusion in the "massacre" at Fort William Henry on Lake George in 1757, British Commander-in-Chief Jeffrey Amherst denied the honors of war to French forces upon the capitulation of Montreal in 1760. On the evening of September 7, 1760, French officers quietly burned the regimental flags they had carried through the difficult campaigns in defense of Canada rather than surrender them to the victorious British.

Chapter 7

The World on Fire

"The volley fired by a young Virginian in the backwoods of America," 18th-century British statesman Horace Walpole observed, "set the world on fire." Two hundred years later, another British statesman, Winston Churchill, recognized the conflict that began with the death of Ensign Jumonville as the first world war. After two years of fighting in North America, the fighting spread to Europe and India in 1756, and to the West Indies, Africa, and the Philippines before the war ended in 1763. Fleets clashed in a far-ranging naval war, and ultimately, the political map of Europe, America, and other parts of the globe was transformed. The Seven Years' War (1756-1763) shaped the second half of the 18th century as profoundly as World War II (1939-1945) did the 20th.

The First Global War

Britain, France, and their European allies viewed the peace that ended the War of the Austrian Succession (1741-1748) as only a temporary truce. Britain and France jockeyed for position overseas, and fighting broke out in North America in 1754. By 1756, the major powers had realigned themselves for the anticipated resumption of war: Britain and Prussia faced France, Austria, and Russia, and both alliances included lesser European powers. A formal declaration of war came in April 1756, when French forces under the Marquis de La Galissonière besieged the British territory of Minorca in the Mediterranean Sea.

The human scale of the European conflict dwarfed the American phase of the war. Armies of more than 100,000 soldiers routinely campaigned in Central Europe, whereas the largest British expeditionary force in North America numbered less than 25,000.

British Prime Minister William Pitt sought to offset France's imposing military strength in Europe by striking forcefully at French colonies in North America, the West Indies, Africa, and India. In 1758, Pitt dispatched expeditions against French trading stations on the west coast of Africa, a rich source of gold dust, ivory, gum arabic, and slaves. Among the human cargo taken aboard British ships during the Seven Years' War was a young girl purchased by the prosperous Wheatley family of Boston. Renamed Phillis by her owners, she learned English and Latin, and became the first published African American poet. "In every human breast," this early advocate of abolitionism wrote, "God has implanted a principle which we call love of freedom. It is impatient of oppression and pants for deliverance." The same sentiment would ring true for colonists just a few years later.

On the Indian subcontinent, British and French trading companies had competed since the 1600s. Periodic conflicts involved private armies raised in Europe by the companies, local indigenous fighters, and a few regular troops and ships. In 1756, fighting broke out in the Bengal region and spread across India over the next six years. By 1761, France had lost its last stronghold, cementing a British colonial domination that would last until 1947.

William Pitt considered the valuable French sugar-producing islands in the West Indies an important part of his strategy to weaken France by seizing her colonies and commerce. In 1759, British expeditions attacked Martinique and Gaudeloupe in the Leeward Islands. Such conquests offered both economic and strategic benefits. They yielded valuable plunder and commodities and created territorial bargaining chips that could offset British losses in Europe in future peace negotiations.

Spain entered the Seven Years' War on the side of France in 1762, prompting British attacks on its colonies in the Leeward Islands and Cuba. The 1762 siege of Havana gave Britain possession of the capital of Spain's American empire, though the human cost to the besieging force from disease was immense. Britain also dispatched an expedition from India that attacked and seized Manila, the principal administrative and commercial center of the Spanish Philippines. British victories on land and sea now ringed the globe.

The Triumph of Britannia

"Our bells are worn threadbare with the ringing of victories," statesman Horace Walpole observed in 1759, as the tide of war turned from France to Britain. Britons on both sides of the Atlantic created a steady demand for commemorative prints, medals, punchbowls, and other objects celebrating British successes.

Britain emerged from the Seven Years' War as the world's leading commercial empire, with newly acquired territories that reached from the Mississippi Valley to India's Ganges River. By the 1763 Treaty of Paris, Britain gained islands in the West Indies and territory in India and Africa, received favorable concessions to British interests in Europe, and became the sole colonial power in North America east of the Mississippi River.

This vast overseas empire was a surprising result of the war. More unexepected to Britons at home and in America was how quickly it unraveled.

A Southeast Prospect of the City of New York, c. 1756-61
Artist unknown
Oil on canvas, 38 x 72-1/2 inches
Collection of The New-York Historical Society

THIS EARLY PAINTING OF NEW YORK includes several French ships captured by British privateers during the French and Indian War.

Robert Clive and Mir Jaffier after the Battle of Plassey, 1757, c. 1760
Francis Hayman
Oil on canvas, 39-1/2 x 50 inches
National Portrait Gallery, London

BRITISH ARTIST FRANCIS HAYMAN PRODUCED THIS STUDY for one of four monumental history paintings commemorating British victories in the Seven Years' War. The image portrays British commander Robert Clive's victory over French and native East Indian forces at the 1757 Battle of Plassey.

THIS SERENE VIEW shows the French trade and slaving post of Goree in West Africa at the time it was seized by a British expedition in December 1758.

Attack on Goree, 29 December 1758, c. 1768
Attributed to Dominic Serres
Oil on canvas, 525 x 820 mm
National Maritime Museum, London, BHC0388

THE BATTLE OF QUIBERON BAY, off the coast of France, destroyed the French fleet based in the port of Brest. Freed from the threat of a French invasion, Britain committed even more forces to overseas campaigns. The British navy's virtual control of the Atlantic Ocean hastened the fall of Canada in 1760.

The Battle of Quiberon Bay, 20 November 1759, 1779
Dominic Serres
Oil on canvas, 114.3 cm x 182.88 cm
National Maritime Museum, London, BHC0400

Britons at home and abroad toasted the worldwide victories of their land and sea forces and those of their principal European ally, Prussia, with alcoholic punch served in ceramic bowls bearing a variety of patriotic inscriptions. Fragments of these vessels have been excavated at New York's Fort Ticonderoga and Williamsburg, Virginia.

Punch Bowl, c. 1759
Liverpool, England
"SucceSs to gen[l] Wolfe"
Tin-glazed earthenware decorated in cobalt, blue, green, yellow, dark manganese, purple, and orange (Fazackerly colors), 4-1/2 x 10-3/8 inches
Historic Deerfield, Inc. acc. number 54.206, Photography Penny Leveritt

Punch Bowl, c. 1756-63
London, England
"SucceSs to the King of PruSsia"
Earthenware, tin-glazed (delft), 3-1/2 x 9 inches
The Colonial Williamsburg Foundation, gift of Mr. and Mrs. Stanley Stone, 1978-121

Fragment of a Punch Bowl, c. 1759
English, artist unknown
Inscribed "SucceSs to gen[l] Amher[st]"
Tin-glazed earthenware, fragment measures 6 x 6 x 1-1/2 inches
Collection of the Fort Ticonderoga Museum

Jack Tar: A British Sailor Toasts the Triumph of Britannia, 1762
Gerry Embleton, 2005
Photograph by Rob Long

Britain's navy had long been the strongest element in the defense of the island kingdom and its overseas colonial empire. During the Seven Years' War, the Royal Navy projected unprecedented military power across the globe. British sailors were often known as "tars" because shipboard work left their clothes coated with the substance, or "Jacks," slang for workers or common laborers. These terms were later joined in the familiar nickname "Jack Tar." Aboard ship, the men of the Royal Navy inhabited a "wooden world," with customs and practices completely alien to their land-dwelling fellow Britons. Ethnically and racially diverse, sailors were generally better fed and paid than soldiers. Life at sea could be dangerous and hard, but opportunities for social and professional advancement were great.

BRITISH COMMEMORATIVE MEDALS were struck with increasing frequency as the tide of the Seven Years' War turned against France. This medal commemorates victories in 1759, which came to be known as the "annus mirabilis" or year of miracles.

Victories of the Year Medal, 1759
Artist unknown
Engraved "90"
Silvered brass, 1-3/4 inches diameter
Private Collection

The Piazza at Havana, c. 1762
Dominic Serres
Oil on canvas, 835 x 1233 mm
National Maritime Museum, London, BHC0418

A BRITISH EXPEDITION under the command of Admiral Sir George Pocock and General George Keppel, the Earl of Albemarle, captured Havana, the capital of Spain's American empire, in 1762. Dominic Serres painted a number of works, including this view of the Piazza at Havana, to commemorate this stunning British victory. Many were engraved and published as prints, helping to solidify the artist's reputation as the preeminent chronicler of the Seven Years' War.

Powder Horn, 1762
Cow horn, wood, and iron pins,
14-3/4 x 4 inches
Collection of William H. Myers

The 9th Regiment of Foot was among the land and sea forces dispatched from Britain to join British and American provincial forces in the 1762 attack on Havana. Peyton's richly engraved powder horn commemorates the embarkation of British forces following the Peace of 1763, which returned Havana to Spanish control in exchange for Florida. The horn is inscribed:

YELVERTON PEYTON • CAP:T
9TH REGT FOOT S.^{T} AUGUSTINE
EAST FLORIDA JEN^{Y} 30TH 1767

THE CITY OF HAVANA ILLUMINATED AT THE
EMBARKATION OF THE BRITTISH TROOPS
JULY THE 7TH 1763

NORTH PORT/PONTO/MORO/APOSTLES BATTERY
SHEPHERDS BATTERY/NEW STORE/REGLIER/
GUNNAMACOA/FUZA

Chapter 8

First Rebels

The surrender of Montreal in September 1760 effectively ended the American conflict between Britain and France, although fighting continued overseas for two more years. Long courted as allies and trading partners, Native Americans were left out of the peace negotiations and faced a foreboding shift in British behavior. "The success of his Majesty's arms this campaign," Indian agent George Croghan warned, "gives rise to an opinion generally received in the Army, that we have conquered the continent. It is true we may say we have beat the French, but we have nothing to boast from the war with the Natives."

Pressed to cut costs, British Commander-in-Chief Jeffrey Amherst abolished customary practices such as gift-giving upon which good relations with independent Indian nations depended. Coupled with unwelcome British garrisons and encroachments by Anglo-Americans, these new policies incited a widespread uprising across the Great Lakes and Ohio Country commonly known as "Pontiac's Rebellion," named after the Ottawa leader who led the 1763 attack on Detroit.

Garrisons Under Siege

During the 1758 Forbes expedition, British and provincial authorities assured local Indian peoples that they only intended to drive the French from Fort Duquesne. The tribes, then, viewed with alarm the construction of a massive brick and stone fortress at the Forks of the Ohio. By 1762, British soldiers, now stationed from the borders of Pennsylvania and Virginia to Wisconsin, seemed unwilling or unable to honor wartime promises to act generously and keep squatters and land speculators away.

In 1763, emboldened by charismatic Delaware Indian visionary Neolin, who encouraged pan-Indian resistance to the British, Ohio Indian warriors surrounded Fort Pitt and attacked smaller posts and frontier settlements. Backcountry Pennsylvanians panicked at the mere rumor of fresh raids. "Every tree is become an Indian for the terrified inhabitants," British Colonel Henry Bouquet observed. Angered by the provincial and imperial governments' inability to protect them, frontier vigilantes killed 20 peaceful Conestoga Indians near Lancaster, Pennsylvania, and threatened Christian Moravian converts at Philadelphia.

Frustrated by their inability to check the warriors' attacks on British garrisons in the west after 1763, British commanders planned drastic countermeasures. Amherst and Bouquet discussed spreading smallpox among warring Ohio Indians, a step that Captain Simeon Ecuyer took independently in June 1763, when he gave blankets and a handkerchief from Fort Pitt's smallpox hospital to two Delaware Indian leaders at a council.

This early attempt at germ warfare, combined with limited access to arms, ammunition, and trade goods, made the Indians' attacks difficult to sustain. With the advance of British and American forces under Colonel Bouquet in the fall of 1764, Delaware, Shawnee, and Ohio Iroquois leaders accepted an offer of peace. Such treaties, and the Royal Proclamation of 1763, which prohibited settlement west of the Allegheny Mountains, temporarily eased relations between Indians and the British empire, but Anglo-American pressure to open western lands to settlement produced new tensions. "The lands between the Allegheny hills and the Ohio," Virginia Governor Francis Fauquier reported in 1766, "are said to be so extremely fine that people will run all risks whether from government or from Indians to take possession and seat themselves on these lands without the least plea of right for doing so."

Having suffered from entanglement in previous conflicts between Europeans, most Indian nations were reluctant to support either the British or American rebels in 1775. Many considered the warring British and Americans akin to a pair of scissors: composed of two sharp knives that should destroy one other when closed, such an instrument only cut what came between. Indians always lost in such contests, the reasoning went, although most eastern nations eventually sided with the British against the greater threat of an expansionist American republic.

Happy While United Medal, 1764
Daniel Christian Fueter
Silver, 55 cm diameter
Bibliothèque et Archives Canada/Library and Archives Canada

SILVER PEACE MEDALS bearing the legend "Happy While United" were used to make peace with various Indian nations in the Great Lakes and Ohio Valley between 1764 and 1766.

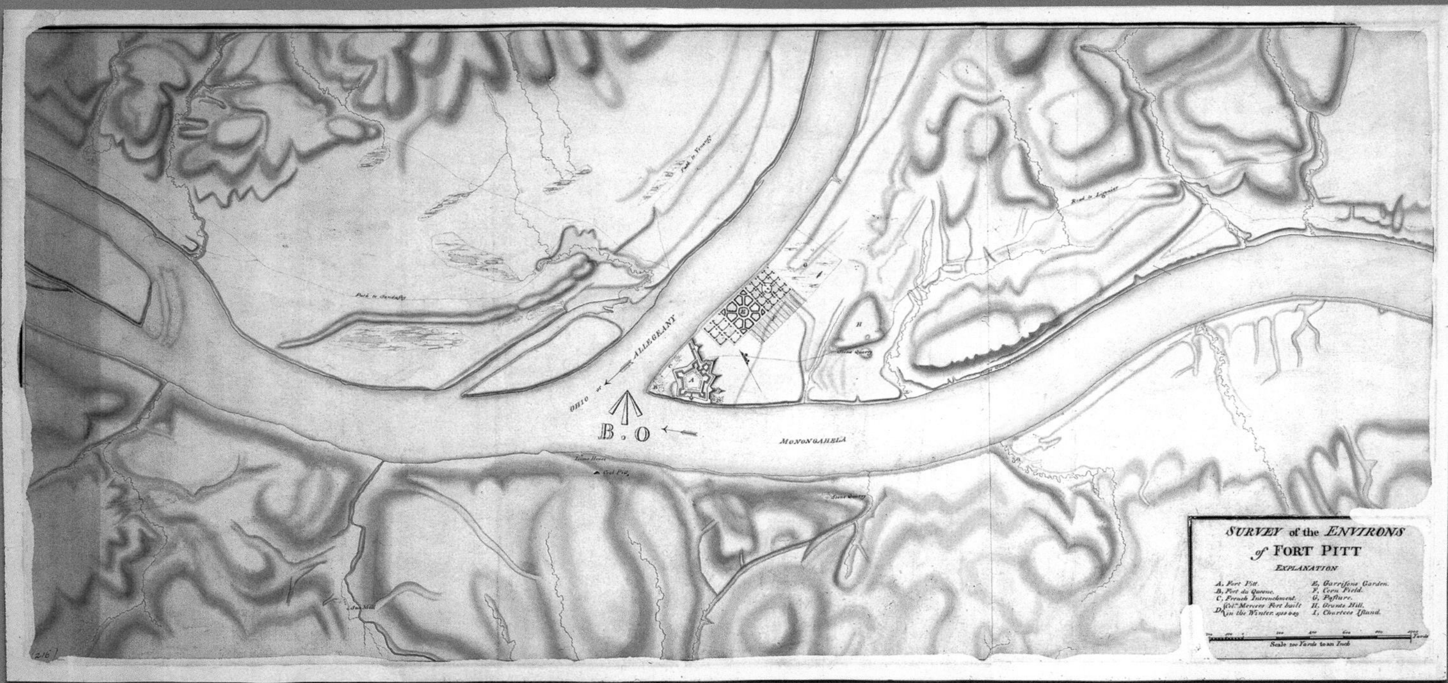

Survey of the Environs of Fort Pitt, c. 1761
Surveyed by Lieut. E Meyer
Ink and watercolor map, 21 x 43 inches
The National Archive of the U.K. TNA: (PRO) ref. WO78/300

British military engineer Elias Meyer produced this detailed survey of the environs of Fort Pitt at the forks of the Ohio River before it was heavily damaged by flooding during the winter of 1762-63. The contrast between the massive earth and brick fortress and the comparatively tiny French Fort Duquesne at the very tip of the confluence (marked "B" on the plan), struck many Ohio Indians as evidence of British intensions to take their lands.

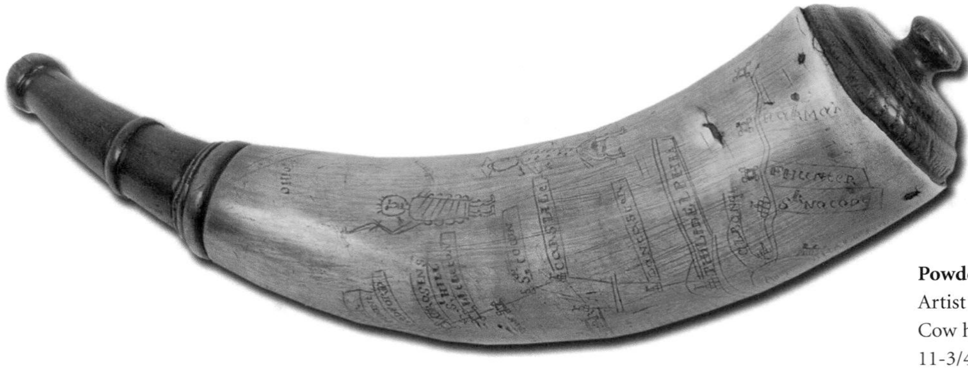

Powder Horn, c. 1759-60
Artist unknown
Cow horn, wood, and iron,
11-3/4 x 3-3/4 inches
Centre County Library and
Historical Museum, Bellefonte,
Pennsylvania

This crudely engraved powder horn attributed to Jonathan Fox, includes depictions of military roads and forts in New York and Pennsylvania, including posts along the Forbes Road from Philadelphia to Pittsburgh. Several stylistically similar powder horns bear dates between 1759 and 1764 and locations in those colonies. They may have been fashioned by a member of the Royal American Regiment (60th), whose members served in campaigns in those regions.

This horn is inscribed:

DIVE ET MONDROIT HONI•SOIT•QUI•MAL•Y•PENESE
PHILIDELPHIA LaNCaSTER CaRSLILE SH TOWN
LouNDON LitLetoN S^{I} HILL CROSINS BEDFORD
AL MOUNT St CreeK L^{O} HILL LagaNeeR PItSBURGH
MONONGAHALaH
ALegaNY

NEW YORK ALBANY S^{K}NaCODy F HUNteR
HaKMa F StaNWIX
HALF MOON S^{T}WatweR SaRatoga F MILLeR
R^{C}B HOUSe

This inkstand belonged to Josiah Franklin Davenport (b. 1727), Benjamin Franklin's nephew, who managed the Pennsylvania provincial trading post at Pittsburgh between 1761 and 1765. He served as a volunteer militia officer during the 1763 siege of Fort Pitt by Ohio Indians.

Inkstand, 1761
Artist unknown
Marked "Fort Pitt/PROVINCE STORE/1761"
"J F DAVENPORT 1761"
Metal, perhaps pewter,
2 x 5-1/3 x 8-1/2 inches
Historical Society of Western Pennsylvania

Joseph Brant (Thayendanegea), 1776
George Romney
Oil on canvas, 127 x 101.6 cm
National Gallery of Canada, Ottawa, Transfer from the Canadian War Memorials, 1921

Mohawk leader Thayendanegea (Joseph Brant), born in the Ohio Country c. 1742-43, was closely associated with British Indian agent William Johnson. He served alongside British forces at Fort Carillon (1758), Niagara (1759), and Montreal (1760). With Johnson's support, Brant attended school in New England before returning to his Mohawk Valley home in 1763. He assisted Johnson in bringing Pontiac's Rebellion to an end and traveled to London in 1776 to seek support against the rebellious American colonists.

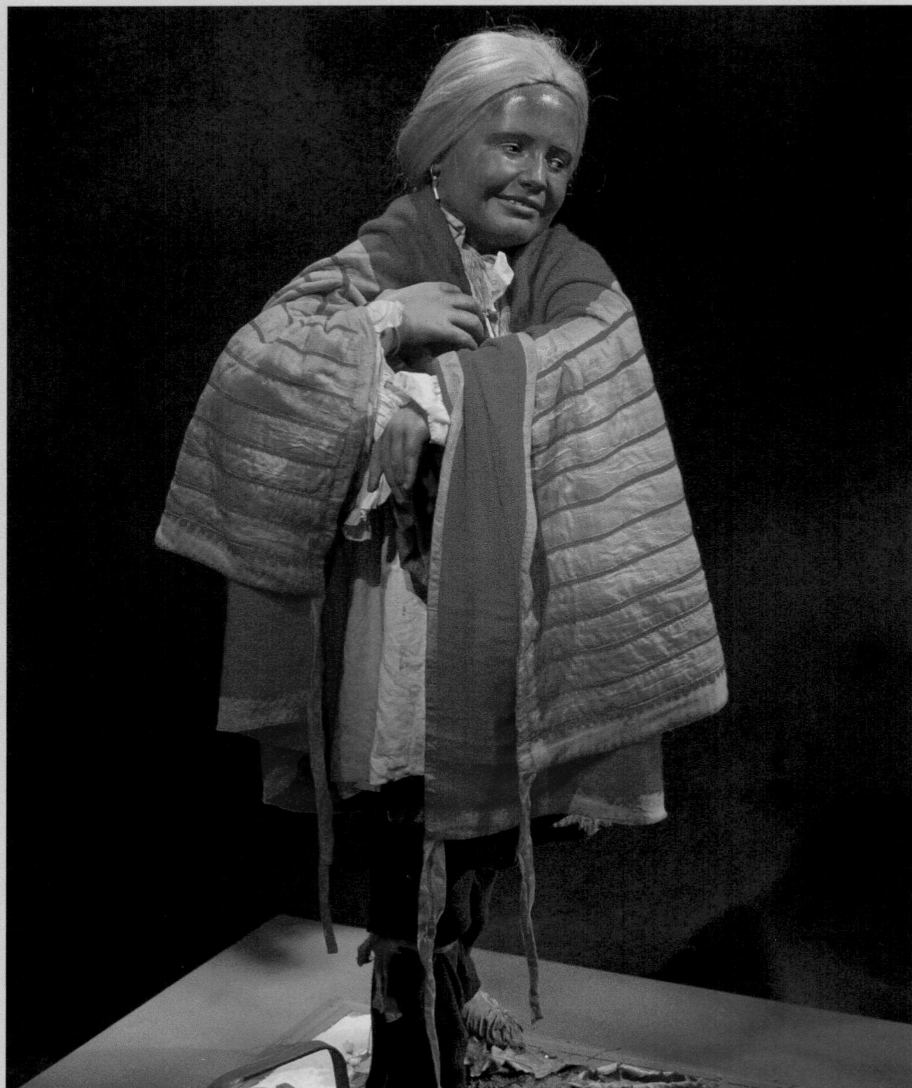

Captive or Kin?: A Pennsylvania Girl in the Ohio Country, 1764
Gerry Embleton, 2005
Photograph by Rob Long

"There is an unknown charm in the Indian life which surprisingly attaches white people," Presbyterian missionary David McClure observed during a trip to the Ohio Country in 1772, "those especially who have been captivated in early life."

Although experiences varied, many captives of European or African descent, particularly those adopted to replace deceased kin, were surprised at the indulgent treatment they received from their captors. Recalling his experience as an adopted member of an Ohio Mohawk family, Pennsylvanian James Smith wrote, "I never knew them to make any distinction between me and themselves in any respect whatever until I left them." After the conclusion of fighting in 1764, British observers were shocked by how attached many captives, including those taken as adults, had become to their captors.

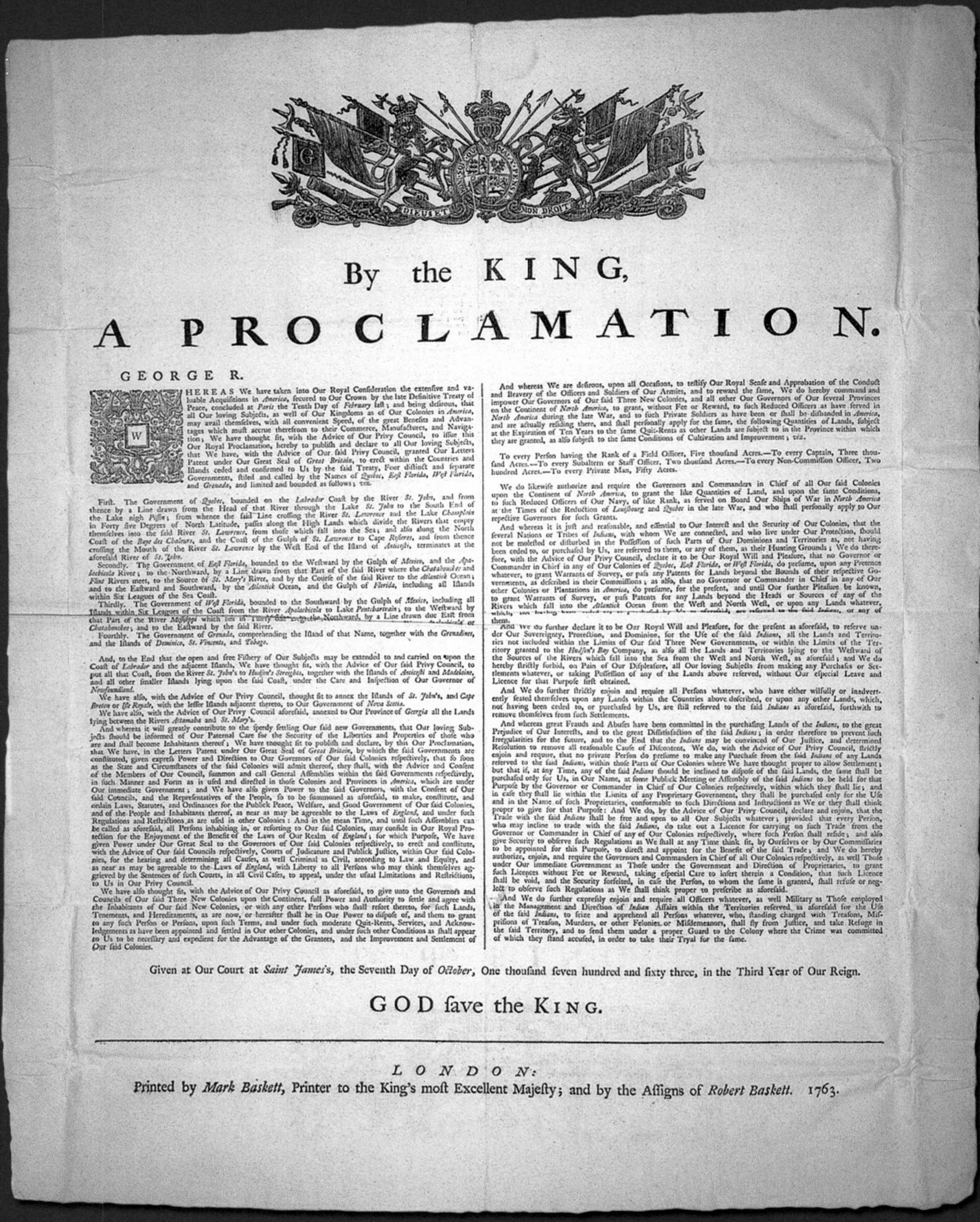

By the KING,

A PROCLAMATION.

GEORGE R.

WHEREAS We have taken into Our Royal Consideration the extensive and valuable Acquisitions in *America*, secured to Our Crown by the late Definitive Treaty of Peace, concluded at *Paris* the Tenth Day of *February* last; and being desirous, that all Our loving Subjects, as well of Our Kingdoms as of Our Colonies in *America*, may avail themselves, with all convenient Speed, of the great Benefits and Advantages which must accrue therefrom to their Commerce, Manufactures, and Navigation; We have thought fit, with the Advice of Our Privy Council, to issue this Our Royal Proclamation, hereby to publish and declare to all Our loving Subjects, that We have, with the Advice of Our said Privy Council, granted Our Letters Patent under Our Great Seal of *Great Britain*, to erect within the Countries and Islands ceded and confirmed to Us by the said Treaty, Four distinct and separate Governments, stiled and called by the Names of *Quebec*, *East Florida*, *West Florida*, and *Grenada*, and limited and bounded as follows; viz.

First. The Government of *Quebec*, bounded on the *Labrador* Coast by the River *St. John*, and from thence by a Line drawn from the Head of that River through the Lake *St. John* to the South End of the Lake nigh *Pissin*; from whence the said Line crossing the River *St. Lawrence* and the Lake *Champlain* in Forty five Degrees of North Latitude, passes along the High Lands which divide the Rivers that empty themselves into the said River *St. Lawrence*, from those which fall into the Sea; and also along the North Coast of the *Baye des Chaleurs*, and the Coast of the Gulph of *St. Lawrence* to Cape *Rosieres*, and from thence crossing the Mouth of the River *St. Lawrence* by the West End of the Island of *Anticosti*, terminates at the aforesaid River of *St. John*.

Secondly. The Government of *East Florida*, bounded to the Westward by the Gulph of *Mexico*, and the *Apalachicola* River; to the Northward, by a Line drawn from that Part of the said River where the *Chatahouchee* and *Flint* Rivers meet, to the Source of *St. Mary's* River, and by the Course of the said River to the *Atlantick* Ocean; and to the Eastward and Southward, by the *Atlantick* Ocean, and the Gulph of *Florida*, including all Islands within Six Leagues of the Sea Coast.

Thirdly. The Government of *West Florida*, bounded to the Southward by the Gulph of *Mexico*, including all Islands within Six Leagues of the Coast from the River *Apalachicola* to Lake *Pontchartrain*; to the Westward by that Part of the River *Mississippi* which lies in Thirty [illegible] Northward, by a Line drawn due East from [illegible] *Apalachicola* or *Chatahouchee*; and to the Eastward by the said River.

Fourthly. The Government of *Grenada*, comprehending the Island of that Name, together with the *Grenadines*, and the Islands of *Dominico*, *St. Vincents*, and *Tobago*.

And, to the End that the open and free Fishery of Our Subjects may be extended to and carried on upon the Coast of *Labrador* and the adjacent Islands, We have thought fit, with the Advice of Our said Privy Council, to put all that Coast, from the River *St. John's* to *Hudson's Streights*, together with the Islands of *Anticosti* and *Madelaine*, and all other smaller Islands lying upon the said Coast, under the Care and Inspection of Our Governor of *Newfoundland*.

We have also, with the Advice of Our Privy Council, thought fit to annex the Islands of *St. John's*, and *Cape Breton* or *Isle Royale*, with the lesser Islands adjacent thereto, to Our Government of *Nova Scotia*.

We have also, with the Advice of Our Privy Council aforesaid, annexed to Our Province of *Georgia* all the Lands lying between the Rivers *Attamaha* and *St. Mary's*.

And whereas it will greatly contribute to the speedy settling Our said new Governments, that Our loving Subjects should be informed of Our Paternal Care for the Security of the Liberties and Properties of those who are and shall become Inhabitants thereof; We have thought fit to publish and declare, by this Our Proclamation, that We have, in the Letters Patent under Our Great Seal of *Great Britain*, by which the said Governments are constituted, given express Power and Direction to Our Governors of Our said Colonies respectively, that so soon as the State and Circumstances of the said Colonies will admit thereof, they shall, with the Advice and Consent of the Members of Our Council, summon and call General Assemblies within the said Governments respectively, in such Manner and Form as is used and directed in those Colonies and Provinces in *America*, which are under Our immediate Government; and We have also given Power to the said Governors, with the Consent of Our said Councils, and the Representatives of the People, so to be summoned as aforesaid, to make, constitute, and ordain Laws, Statutes, and Ordinances for the Publick Peace, Welfare, and Good Government of Our said Colonies, and of the People and Inhabitants thereof, as near as may be agreeable to the Laws of *England*, and under such Regulations and Restrictions as are used in other Colonies: And in the mean Time, and until such Assemblies can be called as aforesaid, all Persons inhabiting in, or resorting to Our said Colonies, may confide in Our Royal Protection for the Enjoyment of the Benefit of the Laws of Our Realm of *England*; for which Purpose, We have given Power under Our Great Seal to the Governors of Our said Colonies respectively, to erect and constitute, with the Advice of Our said Councils respectively, Courts of Judicature and Publick Justice, within Our said Colonies, for the hearing and determining all Causes, as well Criminal as Civil, according to Law and Equity, and as near as may be agreeable to the Laws of *England*, with Liberty to all Persons who may think themselves aggrieved by the Sentences of such Courts, in all Civil Cases, to appeal, under the usual Limitations and Restrictions, to Us in Our Privy Council.

We have also thought fit, with the Advice of Our Privy Council as aforesaid, to give unto the Governors and Councils of Our said Three New Colonies upon the Continent, full Power and Authority to settle and agree with the Inhabitants of Our said New Colonies, or with any other Persons who shall resort thereto, for such Lands, Tenements, and Hereditaments, as are now, or hereafter shall be in Our Power to dispose of, and them to grant to any such Person or Persons, upon such Terms, and under such moderate Quit-Rents, Services, and Acknowledgements as have been appointed and settled in Our other Colonies, and under such other Conditions as shall appear to Us to be necessary and expedient for the Advantage of the Grantees, and the Improvement and Settlement of Our said Colonies.

And whereas We are desirous, upon all Occasions, to testify Our Royal Sense and Approbation of the Conduct and Bravery of the Officers and Soldiers of Our Armies, and to reward the same, We do hereby command and impower Our Governors of Our said Three New Colonies, and all other Our Governors of Our several Provinces on the Continent of *North America*, to grant, without Fee or Reward, to such Reduced Officers as have served in *North America* during the late War, and to such Private Soldiers as have been or shall be disbanded in *America*, and are actually residing there, and shall personally apply for the same, the following Quantities of Lands, subject at the Expiration of Ten Years to the same Quit-Rents as other Lands are subject to in the Province within which they are granted, as also subject to the same Conditions of Cultivation and Improvement; viz.

To every Person having the Rank of a Field Officer, Five thousand Acres.—To every Captain, Three thousand Acres.—To every Subaltern or Staff Officer, Two thousand Acres.—To every Non-Commission Officer, Two hundred Acres.—To every Private Man, Fifty Acres.

We do likewise authorize and require the Governors and Commanders in Chief of all Our said Colonies upon the Continent of *North America*, to grant the like Quantities of Land, and upon the same Conditions, to such Reduced Officers of Our Navy, of like Rank, as served on Board Our Ships of War in *North America* at the Times of the Reduction of *Louisbourg* and *Quebec* in the late War, and who shall personally apply to Our respective Governors for such Grants.

And whereas it is just and reasonable, and essential to Our Interest and the Security of Our Colonies, that the several Nations or Tribes of *Indians*, with whom We are connected, and who live under Our Protection, should not be molested or disturbed in the Possession of such Parts of Our Dominions and Territories as, not having been ceded to, or purchased by Us, are reserved to them, or any of them, as their Hunting Grounds; We do therefore, with the Advice of Our Privy Council, declare it to be Our Royal Will and Pleasure, that no Governor or Commander in Chief in any of Our Colonies of *Quebec*, *East Florida*, or *West Florida*, do presume, upon any Pretence whatever, to grant Warrants of Survey, or pass any Patents for Lands beyond the Bounds of their respective Governments, as described in their Commissions; as also, that no Governor or Commander in Chief in any of Our other Colonies or Plantations in *America*, do presume, for the present, and until Our further Pleasure be known, to grant Warrants of Survey, or pass Patents for any Lands beyond the Heads or Sources of any of the Rivers which fall into the *Atlantick* Ocean from the West and North West, or upon any Lands whatever, which, not having been [illegible] aforesaid, are reserved to the said *Indians*, or any of them.

And We do further declare it to be Our Royal Will and Pleasure, for the present as aforesaid, to reserve under Our Sovereignty, Protection, and Dominion, for the Use of the said *Indians*, all the Lands and Territories not included within the Limits of Our said Three New Governments, or within the Limits of the Territory granted to the *Hudson's Bay* Company, as also all the Lands and Territories lying to the Westward of the Sources of the Rivers which fall into the Sea from the West and North West, as aforesaid; and We do hereby strictly forbid, on Pain of Our Displeasure, all Our loving Subjects from making any Purchases or Settlements whatever, or taking Possession of any of the Lands above reserved, without Our especial Leave and Licence for that Purpose first obtained.

And We do further strictly enjoin and require all Persons whatever, who have either wilfully or inadvertently seated themselves upon any Lands within the Countries above described, or upon any other Lands, which, not having been ceded to, or purchased by Us, are still reserved to the said *Indians* as aforesaid, forthwith to remove themselves from such Settlements.

And whereas great Frauds and Abuses have been committed in the purchasing Lands of the *Indians*, to the great Prejudice of Our Interests, and to the great Dissatisfaction of the said *Indians*; in order therefore to prevent such Irregularities for the future, and to the End that the *Indians* may be convinced of Our Justice, and determined Resolution to remove all reasonable Cause of Discontent, We do, with the Advice of Our Privy Council, strictly enjoin and require, that no private Person do presume to make any Purchase from the said *Indians* of any Lands reserved to the said *Indians*, within those Parts of Our Colonies where We have thought proper to allow Settlement; but that if, at any Time, any of the said *Indians* should be inclined to dispose of the said Lands, the same shall be purchased only for Us, in Our Name, at some Publick Meeting or Assembly of the said *Indians* to be held for that Purpose by the Governor or Commander in Chief of Our Colonies respectively, within which they shall lie; and in case they shall lie within the Limits of any Proprietary Government, they shall be purchased only for the Use and in the Name of such Proprietaries, conformable to such Directions and Instructions as We or they shall think proper to give for that Purpose: And We do, by the Advice of Our Privy Council, declare and enjoin, that the Trade with the said *Indians* shall be free and open to all Our Subjects whatever; provided that every Person, who may incline to trade with the said *Indians*, do take out a Licence for carrying on such Trade from the Governor or Commander in Chief of any of Our Colonies respectively, where such Person shall reside; and also give Security to observe such Regulations as We shall at any Time think fit, by Ourselves or by Our Commissaries to be appointed for this Purpose, to direct and appoint for the Benefit of the said Trade; and We do hereby authorize, enjoin, and require the Governors and Commanders in Chief of all Our Colonies respectively, as well Those under Our immediate Government as Those under the Government and Direction of Proprietaries, to grant such Licences without Fee or Reward, taking especial Care to insert therein a Condition, that such Licence shall be void, and the Security forfeited, in case the Person, to whom the same is granted, shall refuse or neglect to observe such Regulations as We shall think proper to prescribe as aforesaid.

And We do further expresly enjoin and require all Officers whatever, as well Military as Those employed in the Management and Direction of *Indian* Affairs within the Territories reserved as aforesaid for the Use of the said *Indians*, to seize and apprehend all Persons whatever, who, standing charged with Treasons, Misprisions of Treason, Murders, or other Felonies or Misdemeanors, shall fly from Justice, and take Refuge in the said Territory, and to send them under a proper Guard to the Colony where the Crime was committed of which they stand accused, in order to take their Tryal for the same.

Given at Our Court at *Saint James's*, the Seventh Day of *October*, One thousand seven hundred and sixty three, in the Third Year of Our Reign.

GOD save the KING.

LONDON:
Printed by *Mark Baskett*, Printer to the King's most Excellent Majesty; and by the Assigns of *Robert Baskett*. 1763.

Proclamation of 1763
Printed by Mark Baskett, London, printer to the King's most Excellent Majesty; and by the assigns of Robert Baskett
Broadside, 61 x 50 cm
William L. Clements Library, University of Michigan, Ann Arbor

THE PROCLAMATION OF 1763 asserted British imperial control over newly won territories in North America, and sought to reduce tensions with American Indians who had attacked British garrisons throughout the Great Lakes and Ohio Valley.

Chapter 9

The Triumph of Britannia?

After the fall of New France and the stunning victories of the Seven Years' War, British officials turned their attention to the defense and administration of the newly enlarged American empire. For the first time, British leaders had to face the challenges of ruling large numbers of non-Protestant subjects. With 90,000 Catholic subjects in Canada, and at least 50,000 Native Americans (including perhaps 10,000 warriors) living east of the Mississippi River, a large military presence (7,500 regulars) seemed necessary. Rather than burdening British taxpayers, who had footed the enormous costs of the war, Great Britain now expected American colonists to pay for their own defense. At the same time, Parliament enacted a series of measures to centralize colonial administration and enforce trade laws.

Once treated as imperial partners rather than dependents by the wartime administration of William Pitt, many American colonists bristled at what they believed was a systematic effort to deprive them of their British liberties. The burst of pro-British patriotic fervor that had briefly spanned the Atlantic Ocean quickly gave way to protests and recriminations.

Britons or Americans?

The 1765 Stamp Act and the colonial protests that followed have long been viewed as the first steps leading to the American Revolution. The decade that ended in April 1775 with the outbreak of rebellion in Massachusetts would be better characterized as a struggle to define the relationship between mother country and colonies rather than a drive for independence.

The Seven Years' War and its aftermath exposed the widening gap between British and American views. After more than a century's experience of minimal economic and political interference from Britain, many American colonists believed that victory in the Seven Years' War only came when they were treated as equals and asked to contribute soldiers and resources. British officials, on the other hand, tended to recall examples of colonial resistance to British authority and ascribed victory to the British army and navy alone.

Veterans of the French and Indian War filled the armies on both sides of the rebellion that broke out in Massachusetts in April 1775. "These people show a spirit and conduct against us they never showed against the French," British Commander-in-Chief Thomas Gage — a veteran of Braddock's Defeat — observed after the June 1775 Battle of Breed's Hill/Bunker Hill.

George Washington soon took command of the New England forces, drawing on his French and Indian War experiences to forge the "Continental Army." Lessons learned in these early combat experiences continued to influence him after the Declaration of Independence. Faced with a massive British assault on New York that threatened to crush his army and the Revolution, Washington recalled his narrow escapes at Fort Necessity and Braddock's Defeat. "The same Providence that protected us upon those occasions," he wrote fellow veteran Adam Stephen in July 1776, "will, I hope, continue his Mercies, and make us happy Instruments in restoring Peace and liberty to this once favour'd, but now distressed Country."

ECHOES OF THE SEVEN YEARS' WAR

On October 19, 1781, a defeated British army under Lord Cornwallis marched out of Yorktown, Virginia, between lines of jubilant French and American troops. Beyond the horizon, a French fleet in the Chesapeake Bay had sealed the fate of the British force by preventing escape by sea. Led by veterans of the Seven Years' War, the winning forces owed their victory in large part to military reforms undertaken after 1763 by a defeated and humiliated France.

The Franco-American victory at Yorktown led to British recognition of an independent United States of America. In 1794, American armed forces defeated Ohio Indians at the Battle of Fallen Timbers and suppressed a rebellion against the new federal government by Western Pennsylvania "Whiskey Rebels." The struggle to control the Forks of the Ohio River that began with shots fired by Lieutenant Colonel George Washington in 1754 was finally realized 40 years later under President Washington.

ISRAEL PUTNAM (1718-1790) IS REMEMBERED for his famous command, "Don't fire 'til you see the whites of their eyes," issued to American troops before the Battle of Breed's Hill/Bunker Hill in June 1775. After arduous service in the French and Indian War, including the 1762 capture of Havana, Putnam returned to Connecticut and opened a tavern named for British General James Wolfe. Like many American veterans, Putnam took an early and active role in opposing British policies that treated colonists as less than full partners in the empire they had fought so hard for.

Tavern Sign, c. 1768
Artist unknown
Paint on white pine, 30 x 24 1/4 inches
The Connecticut Historical Society Museum,
Hartford, Connecticut

General the Hon. Thomas Gage, 1775
David Martin
Oil on canvas, 82-1/2 x 54 inches
Firle Estate Trustees Settlement

Thomas Gage (c. 1719-1787) commanded the British advanced guard at Braddock's Defeat and was criticized for failing to seize a strategic piece of high ground from which Indian and Canadian fighters poured deadly fire. Gage served through the French and Indian War and raised a regiment of light infantry trained in irregular tactics. He married an American and was appointed commander-in-chief in North America in 1763, a position he held until 1775.

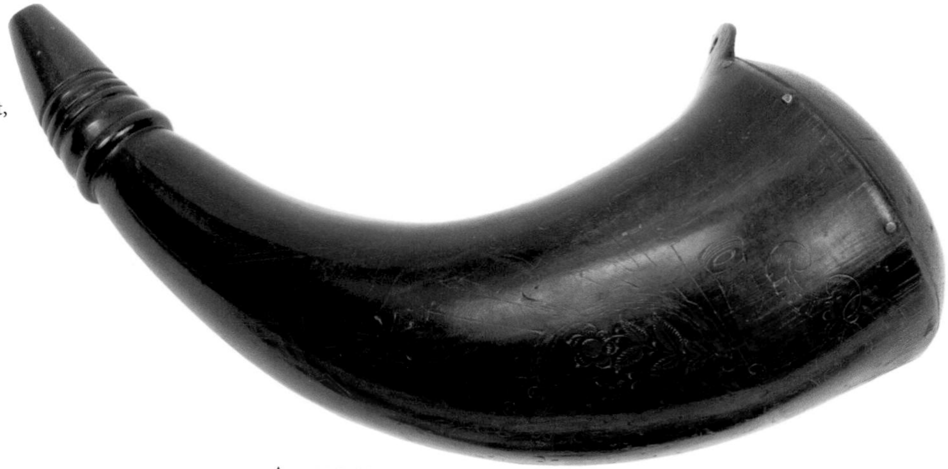

Powder Horn, 1765-70
Inscribed "JS" "Fort Pitt, Ft. Pitt, Aliagheny" "Mana"
American bison horn, wood, brass pins, 9-1/2 x 4-3/4 inches
Collection of Steve Fuller

This striking piece, fashioned from the horn of an American bison, was made by the same artisan who created the Gordon Forbes horn. During the 1760s, British troops used the Ohio River to transport supplies and reinforcements from Fort Pitt to the Illinois country. Travelers noted the presence of "buffalo" (American Bison) within a few days float of Pittsburgh. British troops in the Illinois country consumed large quantities of buffalo meat.

Powder Horn, 1767
Gordon Forbes
Inscribed "Gordon Forbes Esqr. Capt: 34th Regmt: at Fort Chartes Illinois 1767"
Cow horn, wood, brass pins, 13-1/4 x 3-1/2 inches
Collection of Jim and Carolyn Dresslar

Fighting between British and Indian forces in the Great Lakes and Ohio Country in 1763-64 prevented British troops from taking possession of former French posts in the Illinois country until the summer of 1765. Many French inhabitants moved their families and livestock across the Mississippi River to Spanish territory rather than live under British rule. Captain Gordon Forbes (1738-1828) commanded Fort Chartres until 1768, and later served in the American Revolution.

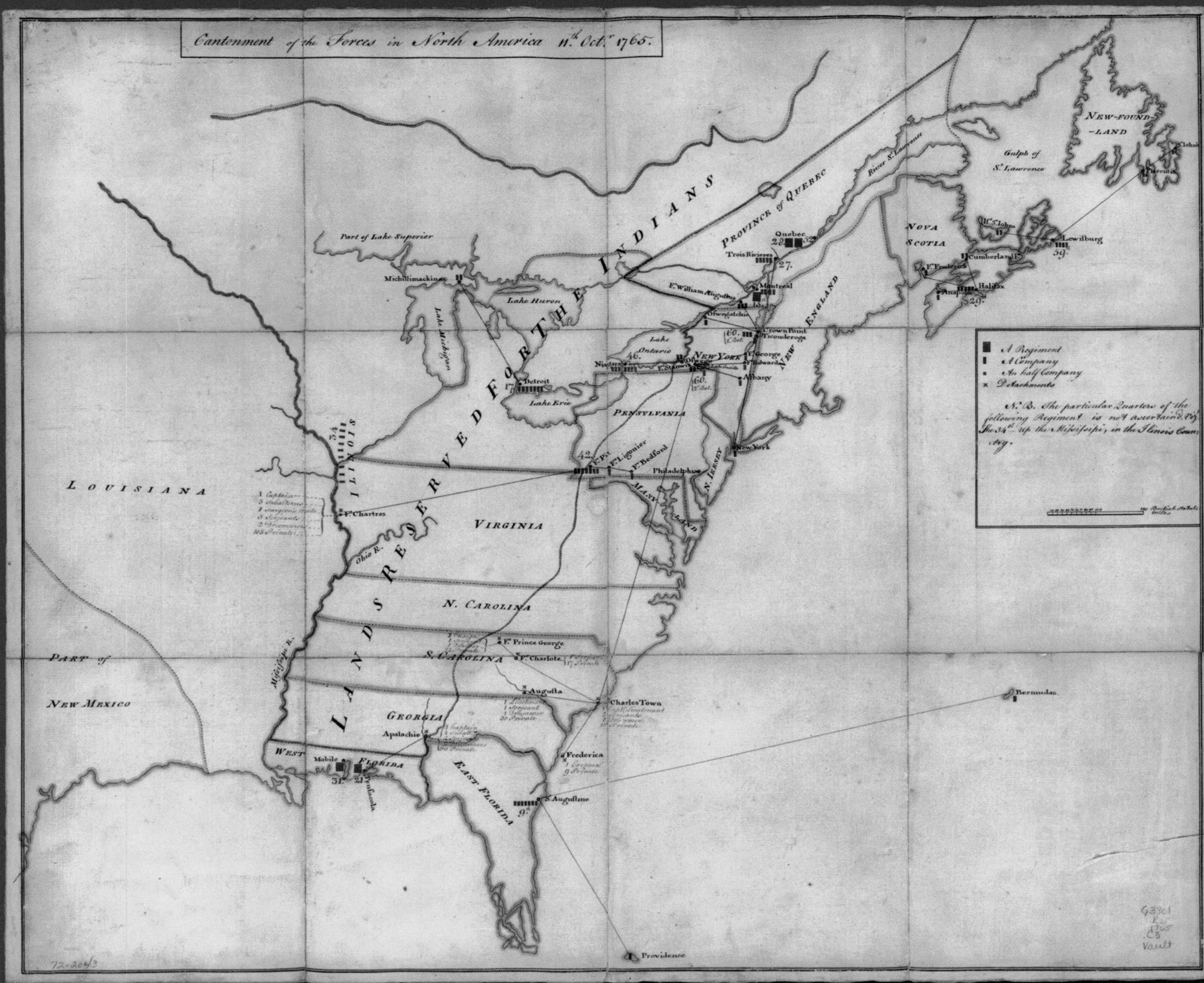

Cantonment of the forces in North America 11th Octr. 1765, 1765
Pen-and-ink and watercolor, 20 x 25 inches
Library of Congress, Geography and Map Division, Washington, D.C.

This map records the location of British forces in North America at the time of the Stamp Act, a tax levied by Parliament to raise funds for the defense of its newly expanded American empire. At this time, troops were concentrated in Canada and in former French and Spanish territory from the Great Lakes to Florida. By the end of the 1760s, a desire to reduce costs and concern about mounting Anglo-American tensions moved British officials to concentrate troops in eastern cities, including Boston, New York, and Philadelphia.

John Philip de Haas, 1772
Charles Willson Peale
Oil on canvas, 50 x 40 inches
National Gallery of Art, Washington, D.C.
Andrew W. Mellon Collection

George Washington in the Uniform of a British Colonial Colonel, 1772
Charles Willson Peale
Oil on canvas, 50-1/2 x 41-1/2 inches
Washington-Custis-Lee Collection,
Washington and Lee University,
Lexington, Virginia

Many British and American veterans of the French and Indian War, including Charles Lee, George Washington, and Israel Putnam, sought land grants as a reward for military service. Dutch immigrant John Philip de Haas led Pennsylvania troops in the French and Indian War and against the Ohio Indians in 1764. After the war, he joined an association of provincial officers who received 24,000 acres in Pennsylvania's Susquehanna Valley. The battle painting on the wall and the sword by his side commemorate de Haas's military service.

Like John Phillip de Haas, with whom he had served on the 1758 Forbes expedition against Fort Duquesne, George Washington chose to commemorate his French and Indian war service when he sat for Charles Willson Peale in 1772.

George Washington, 1776
Charles Willson Peale
Oil on canvas, 44 x 38-5/16 inches
Brooklyn Museum. 34.1178.
Dick S. Ramsay Fund

Washington sat for Peale again in Philadelphia in May 1776. Wearing a uniform modeled on the Fairfax (Virginia) Independent Company that he had helped to equip and train in 1774-75, Washington appears as commander-in-chief of the Continental Army, with Boston (recently evacuated by British troops) in the background.

This British gorget, typical of those worn by regular and some provincial officers during the French and Indian War, was altered during the American Revolution with an engraved "US" for United States. This piece has been traditionally identified as the property of American General Henry Knox, chief of artillery for the Continental Army. Knox was the first secretary of war for the United States, and helped to found the United States Military Academy (West Point).

British Officer's Gorget, c. 1770-1780
Artist unknown
Original Royal coat of arms obliterated
and re-engraved "U S" and
"INIMICA TYRANNIS"
Gilded brass, 5 x 5-1/5 inches
Collection of the Fort Ticonderoga Museum

Chapter 10

Canadians

After the September 1760 surrender of Montreal, British Commander-in-Chief Jeffrey Amherst established a temporary military government in Canada. French troops were shipped off, but fewer than 300 Canadians had the wealth or inclination to leave their homeland. Those who stayed were disarmed and forced to swear allegiance to the British Crown, though they were permitted to retain their property and practice their religion freely. French language and civil law remained in use, and most aspects of social and religious life continued unchanged.

The 1763 Treaty of Paris ended uncertainty about the fate of New France. Absorbed into British North America, the remaining inhabitants from Acadia to the Mississippi Valley were forced to adjust to permanent occupation. Despite British intentions to encourage Protestant settlement and assimilate the Catholic inhabitants, British governors James Murray and Guy Carleton did little to transform the cultural character of Canada, which remained overwhelmingly French.

Charged with securing a province inhabited by more than 70,000 conquered inhabitants and thousands of Native Americans with just a handful of British troops, Governor Carleton advocated lenient rule to win the loyalty of the Canadians. Eyeing the deteriorating political situation in the British colonies to the south, Carleton and British officials realized the province's security depended on Canadian support.

Canada Invaded

Rebellious American colonists invaded Canada in 1775, expecting an easy conquest with the assistance of sympathetic Canadians. But the majority of the French-speaking inhabitants remained neutral in what they considered a dispute between English speakers. In fact, the threat to their homeland and oppressive behavior by the Americans inspired growing numbers of Canadians to take up arms against the invaders. Members of the Canadian militia stood side-by-side with British soldiers and inhabitants to defend Quebec from an American attack on December 31, 1775, and participated in the campaign that drove the invaders away in 1776.

Nearly 40,000 loyal British subjects fled to Canada during and after the American Revolution. Most settled in the Maritime Provinces of Nova Scotia and New Brunswick (formerly Acadia), but about 6,000 entered Quebec and were eventually given land to the west of the settled part of the province, "Upper Canada," now Ontario. This migration planted the seeds of political division between French and English-speaking Canadians that still affect the country's politics today.

An American invasion drove thousands of refugees from the Iroquois Confederacy's homelands as well. Using Fort Niagara as a base, Iroquois warriors under the leadership of Mohawk Joseph Brant, born in the Ohio Country in 1742 and a veteran of the French and Indian War, fought along the New York-Pennsylvania frontier during the American Revolution. In 1784, Brant led Mohawk and other Iroquois refugees to a new settlement on the Grand River in Upper Canada, today the largest Iroquois community in North America.

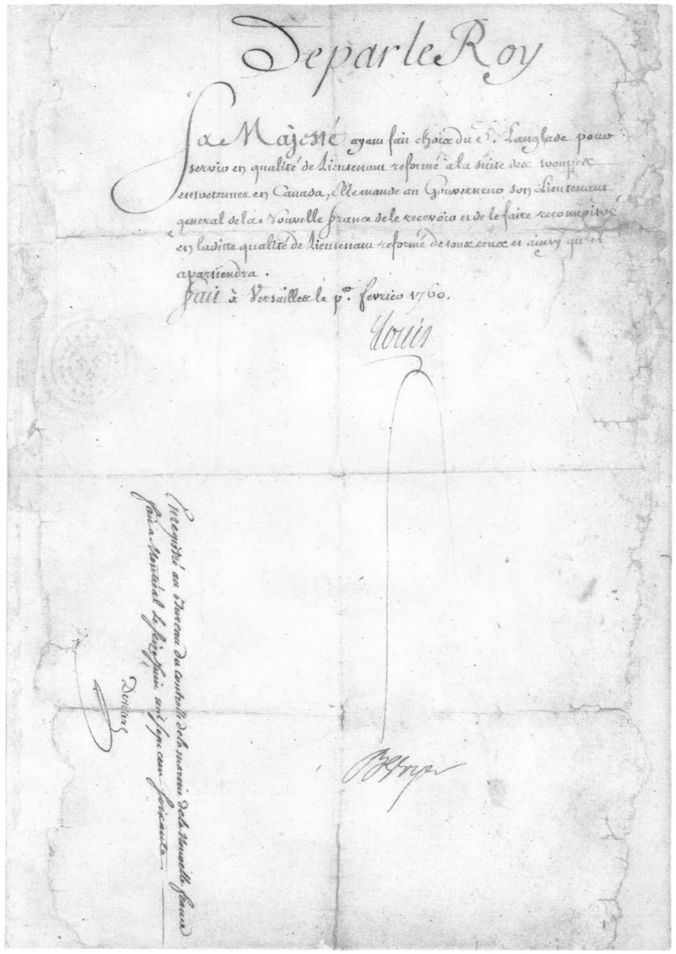

De par le Roy

Sa Majesté ayant fait choix du Sr. Langlade pour servir en qualité de Lieutenant reformé à la suite des troupes entretenues en Canada, Elle mande au Gouverneur son Lieutenant general de la Nouvelle France de le recevoir et de le faire reconnoître en laditte qualité de Lieutenant reformé de tous ceux et ainsy qu'il apartiendra.

Fait à Versailles le 1er fevrier 1760.

Louis

Charles de Langlade's Commission into the French Military, 1760
Artist unknown
Ink on parchment, 36 x 24.6 cm
Neville Public Museum of Brown County

Charles-Michel Mouet de Langlade (1729-1801), son of a Canadian trader and his Ottawa Indian wife, participated in his first battle at age 10. Appointed a cadet in the *Troupes de la Marine* by 1750, Langlade led his Ottawa kinsmen against Miami Indians at Pickawillany (1752) and the British at Fort Duquesne (1755-56), Fort William Henry (1757), Quebec (1759), and Montreal (1760). Langlade received this lieutenant's commission, signed by Louis XV, shortly before the fall of New France.

The Humanity of General Amherst, 1760
Francis Hayman
Oil on canvas, 68.58 x 91.44 cm
The Beaverbrook Foundation,
The Beaverbrook Art Gallery, 1959.92

THIS CANVAS IS A STUDY for one of the four monumental history paintings commemorating British victories in the Seven Years' War that were displayed at the fashionable Vauxhall Gardens near London. The image of a magnanimous Amherst feeding hungry Canadians after the capitulation of Montreal contrasts with the commander's malevolent actions toward American Indians who resisted British control.

Head from a Bust of George III, 1765
Joseph Wilton
Marble, 33 x 26 x 28 cm
McCord Museum of Canadian
History, Montreal

British subscribers contributed funds to purchase two fire engines and a marble bust of King George III for the Canadian citizens of Montreal after a devastating 1765 fire. During the American occupation of Montreal in 1775-76, a mob destroyed the sculpture. In 1834, this fragment was found in a well.

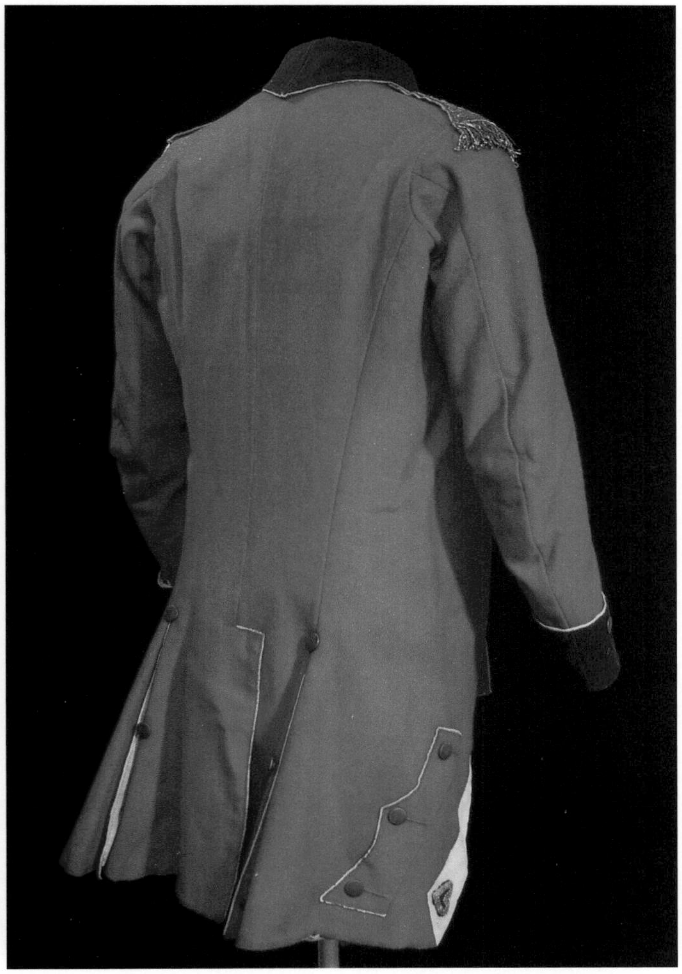

Charles Langlade's British Indian Agency Officer's Coat Front and Back, c. 1775-85
Artist unknown
Wool, linen, metal plated bone or ivory,
92 cm (top of collar to hem) 47.5 (sleeve inseam)
Neville Public Museum of Brown County

OTTAWA-CANADIAN OFFICER CHARLES LANGLADE was commander of the French Fort Michilimackinac when British forces arrived in September 1761. After saving members of the garrison from death during Pontiac's Rebellion, Langlade was employed by the British Indian department. In 1776-77, he helped drive American forces from Canada, and remained a British agent after the American Revolution. In his old age, Langlade enthralled listeners with tales of the 99 battles he claimed to have fought, including Braddock's Defeat.

Colonel Lacorne St.-Luc, date unknown
Artist unknown
Oil on canvas, 29-1/2 x 24-1/2 inches
Library and Archives Canada, (1973-41-1),
Photograph by Alice Lighthall

Canadian officer and merchant St.-Luc de la Corne (c. 1711-1784), also known as Lacorne St.-Luc, was an active partisan leader along the borders of New England during the conflicts of the 1740s and 1750s. He remained in Canada after the British conquest, and was made a member of the legislative council of Quebec in 1775. Like most fellow Canadians, St.-Luc ultimately joined the British to repel the American invaders. He remained a forceful advocate of Canadians' political rights within the British empire.

THE 1774 QUEBEC ACT sought to strengthen French Canadians' acceptance of British rule in the face of American political unrest. The act freed Catholics to participate in governing the province and perpetuated French civil law and Catholic religion. The inscriptions on this reused military gorget may refer to provisions of the Quebec Act. Oneida Indian chief Peter Otsiquette was active during the era of the American Revolution.

Gorget, 18th century
Inscribed "Down with Law and Courts of Quebec / Restore French Law and Roman Catholic Church" and "Otsiquette 1774"
Silver, 4-1/2 x 4 inches
Collection of William H. Myers

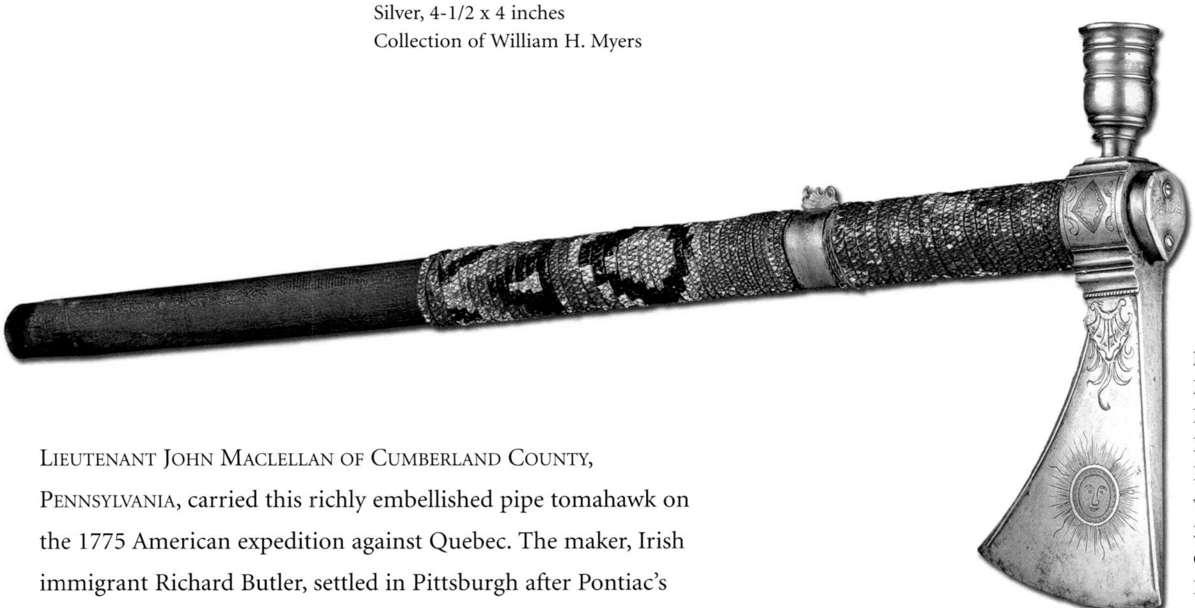

Pipe Tomahawk, c. 1770
Metalwork and handle attributed to Richard Butler
Inscribed "R Butler" and "Lt. J Maclellan"
Iron, steel, silver, pewter, wood, leather, porcupine quills,
21-1/8 x 7-1/4 inches
Collection of Margie and Gordon Barlow
Photograph by John Bigelow Taylor, New York City

LIEUTENANT JOHN MACLELLAN OF CUMBERLAND COUNTY, PENNSYLVANIA, carried this richly embellished pipe tomahawk on the 1775 American expedition against Quebec. The maker, Irish immigrant Richard Butler, settled in Pittsburgh after Pontiac's Rebellion and established himself as a gunsmith and Indian trader. Butler commanded American troops in the Revolution and was killed in 1791 when Ohio Indians defeated an invading American army under General Arthur St. Clair. The porcupine quill decoration on the handle was probably executed by a Shawnee or Iroquois Indian woman living near Pittsburgh.

Exhibit Art and Artifacts

An Expedition to Save New France

Roland-Michel Barrin, Marquis de la Galissonière (1693-1756), oil on canvas, artist unknown, mid-18th century
Stewart Museum, Montreal (Canada), Photography Jasmin Provost

Charles Le Moyne, 2e Baron de Longueuil, oil on canvas, artist unknown, c. 1740
Collection Musée d'art de Joliette, Long term loan of Historical Society of Longueuil

Charles-Jacques Le Moyne, 3rd Baron de Longueuil (1724-1755), oil on canvas, artist unknown, c. 1753
McCord Museum of Canadian History, Montreal, Purchase from Ian Satow, (M985.219)

Marie-Catherine Fleury Deschambault (1740-1818), oil on canvas, artist unknown, c. 1754
Collection Musée d'art de Joliette, Long term loan of Historical Society of Longueuil

Céléron plate, 1749
American Antiquarian Society, Worcester, Mass.

Sundial/compass, Butterfield type, Paris, 1751-1760
Stewart Museum, Montreal, Canada

French military tinned-iron map case
Private Collection

Commission Letter for an Indian chief, Montreal, July 4, 1754
West Overton Museums, Scottsdale, Pennsylvania

Fused glass beads, c. 1752
Jim and Carolyn Dressler

French Trade gun, Tulle, France, ca. 1740-1760
Mr. and Mrs. Earl Lanning

French military musket, model 1728
Charles Thayer

Early French long-shanked M-1729/34 Marine type bayonet
Private Collection

French Serjeant's iron hilted smallsword
Private Collection

French Sergeant's halberd, c. 1730-60
Private Collection

Bayonet, French regulation type, c. 1750-54
Private Collection

French iron-hilted infantry hanger, c. 1690-1730

French brass-hilted naval cutlass, c. 1720-50

French brass-hilted infantry hanger, c. 1720-50
Private Collection

French brass-hilted naval cutlass, c. 1720-50
Private Collection

A People Between

Lapowinsa, oil on canvas, by Gustavus Hesselius, 1735
Atwater Kent Museum of Philadelphia, Historical Society of Pennsylvania Collection

Joseph Brant, oil on canvas, by Ezra Ames, 1806
Fenimore Art Museum, Cooperstown, New York

American Indian and family, oil on canvas, by Benjamin West, 18th century
Hunterian Collection, Hunterian Museum at the Royal College of Surgeons (RCSSC/P249)

Leather Breeches, late 18th century
New-York Historical Society, Gift of Mrs. Samuel M. Stanton

Burden Strap, 18th century
Rock Foundation, New York City

Flintlock Firearm, Bumford Shop, England, c. 1760
The Colonial Williamsburg Foundation, 1981-5

Rifle Barrel Gun, attributed to Andreas Albrecht, Bethlehem or Christian Springs, Penn., c. 1755-65
Mercer Museum of the Bucks County Historical Society, gift of Marshall Ridge, 1922, ACC 10780

Stone Smoking Pipe, mid-18th century
Steve Fuller

Wooden gunpowder cask, 18th century
Private Collection

Pipe tomahawk, dated 1758
Steve Fuller

Pipe Tomahawk, dated 1761, inlayed"F P LECOMPE" and "A. LEPOIVRES"
Steve Fuller

Trade shirt, c. 1780
Canadian Museum of Civilization

Garter, 18th century

Pouch, 18th century
The Field Museum, Gift of Mrs. A. W. F. Fuller, 1965, #2890.82734, #2841.258665 (garter and pouch)

*Glass bead wampum belt, North-East Iroquois, mid-18th century

Woven wool yarn sash, North-East Iroquois, mid-18th century

Woven glass bead leg bands, 18th century
Peter the Great Museum of Anthropology and Ethnography (Kunstkamera) of the Russian Academy of Sciences, 1901-13, 1901-22, 1901-15 (belt, sash, and leg bands)

Leggings, 18th century
Livrustkammaren, invnr 20643-44 (45/56 b), Stockholm, Sweden

*Green wool leggings with ribbon and bead decoration, mid-18th century
Peter the Great Museum of Anthropology and Ethnography (Kunstkamara) of the Russian Academy of Sciences, 1901-3A and 1901-3B

Moccasins, 18th century
National Museum of the American Indian, Smithsonian Institution, Washington, D.C., 19/6364

*Wool blanket fragment with ribbon and bead decoration, northeastern North America mid-18th century
Peter the Great Museum of Anthropology and Ethnography (Kunstkamera) of the Russian Academy of Sciences, 1901-5

Plaited Quillwork Strap, Great Lakes region, 18th century
Rock Foundation, New York City

Wampum Belt, late 17th or 18th century
National Museum of the American Indian, Smithsonian Institution, Washington, D.C., photography by David Heald, 5/3150

French Peace Medal, by Jean Duvivier (Reign of Louis XV)
Library and Archives Canada, (PAC H1253)

British Peace Medal, early 18th century (Reign of George II)
Collection of Fort Ticonderoga Museum

Calumet pipe, 18th or early 19th century
Rock Foundation, New York City

Woven garter, eastern North America, 18th or early century
Rock Foundation, New York City

Pipe bag, northeastern North America, 18th or early 19th century
Rock Foundation, New York City

Gorget, c. 1750
William H. Myers

*Woven garters, 18th century
Peter the Great Museum of Anthropology and Ethnography (Kunstkamara) of the Russian Academy of Sciences

Woven belt pouch, 18th century
Field Museum of Natural History, Chicago

Woven sash, 18th century
Field Museum of Natural History, Chicago

*Woven sash, 18th century
Peter the Great Museum of Anthropology and Ethnography (Kunstkamara) of the Russian Academy of Sciences

*Woven sash, 18th century
Peter the Great Museum of Anthropology and Ethnography (Kunstkamara) of the Russian Academy of Sciences

The Storm Rising in the West

Colonel Abraham Barnes, oil on canvas, by John Wollaston, 1753-54
Corcoran Gallery of Art, Washington, D.C., Museum Purchase, Gallery Fund and gift of the Honorable Orme Wilson

A Charming Field for an Encounter, oil on canvas, by Robert Griffing, 2002
National Park Service, Fort Necessity National Battlefield

Pipe tomahawk, engraved "I. Fraser," c. 1750-60
Steve Fuller

Military frock coat, mid-18th century
Collection of the Vigo County Historical Society and Museum, Terre Haute, Indiana

Journal of Major George Washington (Williamsburg: William Hunter), 1754
Special Collections, John D. Rockefeller, Jr. Library, Colonial Williamsburg Foundation

Commission: Gov. Robert Dinwiddie appoints Daniel Parke Custis as lieutenant in Virginia militia, ink on vellum with wafer seal, 1754
Special Collections, John D. Rockefeller, Jr. Library, Colonial Williamsburg

George Washington to James Hamilton, April 27, 1754
Darlington Library, University Library System, University of Pittsburgh

George Washington to Robert Dinwiddie, May 29, 1754
Darlington Library, University Library System, University of Pittsburgh

Treaty of Fort Necessity, 3 July 1754
Royal Ontario Museum. Gift of Dr. Sigmund Samuel

The Great Warpaths

Lieutenant Colonel Nathan Whiting, oil on canvas, attributed to John Durand, c. 1768
The Connecticut Historical Society Museum, Hartford, Connecticut

General Johnson Saving a Wounded French Officer, oil on canvas, by Benjamin West, c. 1764-1768
Derby Museums and Art Gallery, UK

Lieutenant General James Abercromby, oil on canvas, by Allan Ramsay, c. 1760
Collection of the Fort Ticonderoga Museum

Halberd tomahawk, 18th century
Mr. and Mrs. Earl Lanning

British shot pouch, c. 1755
Collection of Charles Thayer

Powder horn, 1748
Collection of Jim and Carolyn Dressler

Powder horn, attributed to John Bush, 1756
The Connecticut Historical Society Museum, Hartford, Connecticut

Wine cup, engraved with the coat-of-arms of Louis-Joseph Montcalm, Marquis de Montcalm, 18th century
McCord Museum of Canadian History, Montreal, Gift of David Ross McCord

Wrist plate, British Land Pattern 1730 musket, (issued 1754)

Early British Land Pattern bayonet, engraved "50th Rt./f/32," 1740s (issued 1754)

Early British Land Pattern bayonet, engraved "SWP/2/No. 2" 1740s (issued 1754)
Private Collection

Mortar shell fragments and burned iron nails
James B. Richardson III

Iron axe and grape shot
James B. Richardson III

French Model 1716 bayonet, 1758
Private Collection

Mourning pendant, 1758
Collection of the Ft. Ticonderoga Museum

Fort Carillon powder horn, 1759
James B. Richardson III

Lieutenant Jabez Thompson's powder horn, 1757
William H. Myer

*Dutch flat-bladed bayonet, c 1720-50
Private Collection

*Dutch long-shanked bayonet, c 1715-30
Private Collection

*Dutch Military Musket, c. 1700-1720
The West Point Museum United States Military Academy

British Land Pattern 1730 musket
Private Collection

British Land Pattern 1742 musket
Private Collection

Wristplate from a British Land Pattern musket, c. 1755-1776
Private Collection

British "Crown 5" Land Pattern bayonet, c. 1755-57
Private Collection

British officer's fusil, c. 1759
Private Collection

British iron-hilted infantry hanger, c. 1755-60
Private Collection

The Backcountry War

Major General Braddock, oil on canvas, by Robert Connell, 2002
Robert Connell

Scarouady, oil on canvas, by Robert Connell, 2002
Robert Connell

British semi basket hilt sword, c.1755
Private Collection

Stove Plate, inscribed "DIS IST DAS JAHR DARIN WITET" (This is the year in which rages), 1756
Collection of the Moravian Historical Society, Nazareth, Pennsylvania

Colonel Edward Fell (1737-1766), oil on canvas, attributed to John Hesselius, c. 1764
The Maryland Historical Society, Baltimore, Maryland

Henry Bouquet, by John Wollaston, c. 1758
Atwater Kent Museum of Philadelphia, Historical Society of Pennsylvania Collection

Colonel George Washington, oil on canvas, by Robert Connell, 2002
Robert Connell

*Holster pistols, by James Barbar (1st), 1755
Private Collection

War club, ball-head style, mid-18th century
Steve Fuller

War club, sword-style, early 18th century
Jim and Carolyn Dressler

Moccasins, c. 1792-96
National Museum of the American Indian, Smithsonian Institution, Washington, D.C. 24/2014

Knife and sheath, late 18th century
National Museum of the American Indian, Smithsonian Institution, Washington, D.C. 3/2873

Burden strap, 18th century
Rock Foundation, New York City

Powder horn, c. 1759-60
Canadian War Museum Collection

Powder horn, inscribed "John Pembarton,"1758
William H. Myers
Powder horn, marked "PATT WALSH ENs OF MAJr GENL LYMANS REGT 1757"
Huntington Museum of Art, Huntington, West Virginia, bequest of Herman P. Dean
Prisoner cord, 18th century
Rock Foundation, New York City
Burden strap, 18th century
Rock Foundation, New York City
Erzehlung von den Trubsalen und der Wunderbahren Befreyung so geschehen an William Flemming und dessen Weib Elisabeth, Lancaster (Pennsylvania), 1756
Darlington Library, University Library System, University of Pittsburgh
French and Indian Cruelty; Exemplified in the Life... of Peter Williamson, 1757
Darlington Library, University Library System, University of Pittsburgh
Kittanning Medal, 1756
Collection of City of Fredericksburg, loan facilitated by APVA Preservation Virginia and the Hugh Mercer Apothecary Shop
Powder horn, map engraved showing Fort Duquesne, c.1759-60
The Mariners' Museum, Newport News, Virginia
British officer's gorget, c. 1750
Private Collection
Humphrey Bland, Treatise of Military Discipline, 1747
The George C. Neumann Collection, a gift of the Sun Company to Valley Forge National Historical Park
British brass-hilted infantry smallsword, c. 1730-1760
Private Collection
Smooth rifle, c. 1750-60
Collection of the Moravian Historical Society, Nazareth, Pennsylvania
*Highland officer's backsword, c. 1740-60
Private Collection
Pair of flintlock pistols, c. 1760
By John Murdoch, Doune, Scotland
Trustees of the Royal Armouries. Leeds, England, XII.1673&1674
*Highland Pistol, signed "William Allan," c. 1750-60
Private Collection
*Camp knife and three-tined fork, undated
Mount Vernon Ladies' Association, Gift of Lieutenant Alexander Rogers, through his father Colonel Alexander Rogers
Plate, marks of Robert Porteous, London, undated
Mount Vernon Ladies Association, Gift of Dr. and Mrs. Joseph E. Fields
Deed of Indian Chiefs to Settlers in the Wyoming Valley of Pennsylvania, July 11, 1754
Darlington Library, University Library System, University of Pittsburgh
Friendly Association peace medal, 1757
Atwater Kent Museum of Philadelphia, Historical Society of Pennsylvania Collection
Draft Animal Shoes, Vehicle Hardware, c. 1755
James B. Richardson III, Douglas Angeloni, and the Historical Society of Western Pennsylvania
Dunbar's Camp Debris, c.1755
James B. Richardson III, Douglas Angeloni, and the Historical Society of Western Pennsylvania

THE FIGHT FOR CANADA

Marquis de Boishébert (1727-1797), oil on canvas, artist unknown, c. 1753
McCord Museum of Canadian History, Montreal; Purchase from Madame Rolland
Portrait of an Unidentified British Officer, oil on canvas, by John Wollaston, c. 1749-69
Tryon Palace Historic Sites and Gardens, New Bern, North Carolina
Medal, Order of Saint-Louis, c. 1775-1825
McCord Museum of Canadian History, Montreal (M966.22)
Medal, "Cumberland Society," 1746
Private Collection
Medal, "The Loyal and Friendly Society of the Blew and Orange", c. 1727-60
Private Collection
Dirk, inscribed "Ja. Tompson," date unknown
Dirk, inscribed with Masonic symbol, date unknown
Canadian War Museum Collection
British basket-hilted backsword, c. 1757
Private Collection
Manuscript order, signed by Admiral Charles Hardy, 1758
Private Collection
Troopboat, c. 1758
National Maritime Museum, London, Greenwich Hospital Collection
The Intendant's Palace, Quebec, oil on canvas, Dominic Serres, 1760
The Beaverbrook Art Gallery, Purchased with funds from a Minister of Communications Cultural Property Grant and the General Purchase Fund, 1992.01
The Bishop's House with the Ruined Town of Quebec, the St. Lawrence Beyond, oil on canvas, by Dominic Serres, 1760
The Beaverbrook Art Gallery, Purchased with the funds from a Minister of Communications Cultural Property Grant and the General Purchase Fund, 1992.02
A View of the Treasury and Jesuits College, Quebec City, Quebec, oil on canvas, by Dominic Serres, 1760
Bibliothéque et Archives du Canada/Library and Archives Canada
A View of the Church of Notre-Dame-de-la-Victoire, Quebec City, Quebec, oil on canvas, by Dominic Serres, 1760
Bibliothéque et Archives Canada/Library and Archives Canada
The Death of Wolfe, oil on canvas, artist unknown, c. 1770-1774
The Colonial Williamsburg Foundation
Cannon ball from Fort Levi, c. 1760
James B. Richardson III
Sir Jeffery Amherst (1717-1797), oil on canvas, by Joshua Reynolds, 1765
Mead Art Museum, Amherst College, Amherst, Massachusetts, Museum Purchase, AC 1967.85
Great Lakes Indian garters and pouch, c. 1760
The Field Museum, gift of Mrs. A.W.F. Fuller, 1964, (2820.15559) and (2820.155563)
Medal, by Daniel Christian Fueter, 1761
Library and Archives Canada

THE WORLD ON FIRE

The Battle of Quiberon Bay, 20 November, 1759, oil on canvas, by Nicholas Pocock, 1812
National Maritime Museum, London
Attack on Goree, 29 December, 1758, oil on canvas, attributed to Dominic Serres, (1719-1793)
National Maritime Museum, London, BHC0388
British iron-hilted naval cutlass, c. 1745-1760
Private Collection
British silver-hilted officer's spadroon,William Kinman, London, 1761
Private Collection
The Piazza at Havana, oil on canvas, by Dominic Serres, (1719-1793)
National Maritime Museum, London
Powder horn, 1767
William H. Myers
Powder horn, c. 1763-64
William H. Myers
Commemorative medal, "Louisbourg Taken," reverse, 1758
Private Collection
Award medal, "Louisbourg Taken," observe, 1758
Private Collection
Medal "Victories of the Year," 1758
Private Collection
Medal, "Victories of the Year" 1759
Private Collection
Medal, "Quebec Taken" by Thomas Pingo, c. 1759-60
McCord Museum of Canadian History, Montreal
Halfpenny with trophy of arms and thistle, 1762
Private Collection
Medal, "Belle Isle taken," 1761
Private Collection
Medal, "British commanders," 1759
Private Collection
Punch bowl, inscribed "Success to the British Arms," London, England, c. 1756-63
The Colonial Williamsburg Foundation, Gift of Mr. and Mrs. Stanley Stone, 1978-122
Punch bowl, inscribed "Success to the King of Prussia," maker unknown, London England, c. 1756-63
The Colonial Williamsburg Foundation
Punch bowl, maker unknown, Liverpool, England, c. 1756-63
Colonial Williamsburg
Fragment of a punch bowl, inscribed "Success to Genl Amherst," c. 1758-60
Collection of the Fort Ticonderoga Museum
Punch bowl, inscribed "Success to genl Wolfe," London, England, c. 1759
Historic Deerfield, Inc., acc. number 54.206.
Punch bowl, inscribed "Rouse up Bold Brittons fa'm'd of OLD/ your powerfu'll Arms advance/ Nere let the Shamefull tale be told/you Subjecks were to France," c. 1765
Winterthur Museum, Gift of Mrs. Nancy du Pont Reynolds
Plate, "Success to the King of Prussia and His Forces," 1756-63
Winterthur Museum, Gift of Mr. and Mrs. John Mayer
Medal, "British commanders," 1759
Private Collection

FIRST REBELS

Powder horn, 1764
Canadian Museum of Civilization
*Forbes Road powder horn
Margie and Gordon Barlow
Forbes Road powder horn, c. 1759-64
Centre County Library and Historical Museum, Bellefonte, Pennsylvania
Inkstand, marked "J F DAVENPORT/ FORT PITT/ PROVINCE STORE/ 1761," 1761
Historical Society of Western Pennsylvania, Gift of anonymous donor, 2003.60
Caesar and his son at Pittsburgh, 1776, by Robert Connell, 2000
Robert Connell
Peace medal, by Daniel Christian Fueter, 1764
National Library and Archives Canada
*Glass bead wampum belt, Northeastern North America, mid-18th century
Peter the Great Museum of Anthropology and Ethnography (Kunstkamara) of the Russian Academy of Sciences, 1901-10
*Glass bead wampum pouch, northeastern North America, mid-18th century
Peter the Great Museum of Anthropology and Ethnography (Kunstkamara) of the Russian Academy of Sciences, 1901-6
*Glass bead wampum cuffs, northeastern North America, mid-18th century
Peter the Great Museum of Anthropology and Ethnography (Kunstkamara) of the Russian Academy of Sciences,1901-7
*Lead shot, gun flints, lice comb, pins, button, thimble from Fort Pitt Blockhouse, late18th century
Fort Pitt Society of The Daughters of the American Revolution

THE TRIUMPH OF BRITANNIA?

Powder horn, Inscribed "JS" "Fort Pitt, Ft. Pitt, Aliagheny, Mana" 1765-70
Collection of Steve Fuller
Powder horn, Pickelata, 1765
American Antiquarian Society, Worcester, Mass.
Powder horn, inscribed "Gordon Forbes Esqr. Capt: 34th Regmt: at Fort Chartes Illinois 1767," 1767
Jim and Carolyn Dressler
Powder horn, Fort William Augustus, 1763
William H. Myers
Tavern sign, artist unknown, c. 1768
The Connecticut Historical Society Museum, Hartford, Connecticut
*John Phillip De Haas, oil on canvas, by Charles Willson Peale, 1772
National Gallery of Art, Washington, D.C.,
George Washington land survey, 1771-72
Darlington Library, University Library System, University of Pittsburgh
*Surveyor's compass, maker unknown, date unknown
Mount Vernon Ladies' Association, Gift of Judge Charles Burgess Ball, great-grandson of Colonel Charles Washington, brother of George Washington, 1876
Bullet mold, owned by Israel Putnam, c. 1750s
William H. Guthman
Powder horn, 1756
James E. Routh, Jr
British or American silver-hilted smallsword, c. 1750-60
St. Andrews Society of Philadelphia
British officer's gorget, attributed to Henry Knox, c. 1760-70
Collection of the Fort Ticonderoga Museum

CANADIANS

The Humanity of General Amherst, oil on canvas, by Francis Hayman, 1760
The Beaverbrook Foundation, The Beaverbrook Art Gallery, 1959.92
Silk officer's sash, c. 1750-75
The Connecticut Historical Society Museum, Hartford Connecticut
*Pipe tomahawk, inscribed "Richard Butler, Lt Maclellen" c. 1770
Collection of Margie and Gordon Barlow, photography by John Bigelow Taylor, NYC
Head from a bust of George III, by Joseph Wilton, 1765
McCord Museum of Canadian History, Montreal
Gorget, inscribed "Down with Law and Courts of Quebec / Restore French Law and Roman Catholic Church" and "Osiquette 1774," mid- to late 18th century
William H. Myers
Woodland Indian bag, 18th century
Wyck, An Historic House and Garden, Philadelphia
Pennsylvania Longrifle, c. 1765-1775
Mr. and Mrs. Earl Lanning
Charles de Langlade's Commission in the French military, 1760
Neville Public Museum of Brown County
British Indian Agency Officer's Coat
Neville Public Museum of Brown County

*Denotes items that appeared in Pittsburgh only

THE MAKING OF AN EXHIBIT

A Tale Worthy of Antiques Roadshow

BY R.S. STEPHENSON

As hundreds of objects and artworks arrived in Pittsburgh in the months leading up to the opening of *Clash of Empires*, one of the most common questions from colleagues and visitors was "How in the world did you find all this stuff?" The answer is complex, because some of the pieces in *Clash* are old friends I've known for years, like the University of Pittsburgh's George Washington letters that I first saw as a high school student. Other objects, like the magnificent painting by Benjamin West that graces the cover of this catalog, I've long admired from afar. Many important pieces I had only seen as fuzzy black-and-white photos in old journal articles or exhibit catalogs. But people seem to be most intrigued by the accidental discoveries that came along the way. There is no better illustration of the role that serendipity played in bringing *Clash of Empires* to life than the interlocking stories of an American Indian pouch from a Quaker House in Philadelphia and a silver-mounted sword from the French and Indian War era that drew blood in a famous Revolutionary War battle.

Germantown, in northwest Philadelphia, retains a striking collection of carefully preserved and restored 18th-century homes. About 10 years ago, a tip on the whereabouts of an early Pennsylvania rifle led me to Wyck, home to nine generations of a Quaker family and now a historic house museum with a rich collection of early furniture and decorative arts. The rifle proved to be something else entirely, but Curator Betsy Solomon graciously toured me around the splendid house and collection. I was particularly taken with a small, well-preserved group of eastern American Indian items from the early 19th century. We lingered over a single moccasin finely decorated with dyed porcupine quills and tiny sheet metal cones arranged along the edges of the cuffs. Little did I know how important those cones would become.

Like many historic house museums in Germantown (and indeed, throughout the United States), Wyck is blessed with an active board that includes descendents of the people who occupied the property during the two-and-a-half centuries that it was a family home. A couple of years after my visit, a box filled with odds and ends — mostly small 19th-century pieces inherited by a board member whose mother was a Wyck descendent — arrived on Betsy Solomon's desk. Among them was a rough wool shoulder bag decorated with white glass beads that the donor thought might have been a woman's purse from the 1920s. When she looked the piece over, however, Betsy spotted something odd — two clusters of fringe with the same kind of rolled sheet metal cones that she remembered from the moccasins we'd looked at together.

A quick trip up to Wyck from my home in Delaware confirmed what Betsy suspected — the pouch was much older, and American Indian-made. Stylistic comparisons with other examples collected between 1750 and 1780 suggest it was probably made in the New York-Pennsylvania region, home to numerous native peoples including the Delaware, Munsee, Mahican, and Mohican, as well as the Six Nations of the Iroquois Confederacy (Mohawk, Oneida, Onondaga, Cayuga, Seneca, and Tuscarora). We're still searching for clues about its precise origin and descent, but are delighted to publicly exhibit for the first time such a rare and beautiful example of an American Indian woman's work.

About two months before the exhibit opening in Pittsburgh, I got a call from Jim Bishop in Philadelphia. Jim is a board member at Wyck, and, he explained, had recently heard that the Indian pouch was going to be loaned to the *Clash of Empires* exhibition. In addition to his work on behalf of Wyck, Jim is president of the St. Andrews Society of Philadelphia, a charitable organization founded in the 1740s to assist distressed Scottish immigrants. Over the past two-and-a-half centuries, the still-active society has amassed a fascinating collection of objects, books, and manuscripts, including, Jim informed me, a sword with an interesting history.

Jim asked if I had ever heard of a fellow named Hugh Mercer. I had. Mercer (1726-1777) was a Scottish physician who immigrated to Philadelphia after backing the losing side in a 1745-1746 uprising against the reigning British monarch, the Hanoverian King George II. Following the defeat of the mostly Scottish rebels at the Battle of Culloden, Mercer and other followers of "Bonnie" Prince Charles Edward Stuart fled to the American colonies. When the French and Indian War broke out in Pennsylvania in 1755, Mercer raised a company of provincial soldiers and served on the frontier west of the Susquehanna River. In September 1756, he was wounded during an attack on the Delaware Indian town of Kittanning, located 40 miles north of the French Fort Duquesne. This was one of the few successful offensive

Woodland Indian Bag, 18th century
Courtesy of Wyck, An Historic House and Garden, Philadelphia

operations undertaken by American colonial troops against the French and their Indian allies during the early years of the conflict. In recognition of this service, the city of Philadelphia presented each of the officers with a silver commemorative medal — the first American-made military decoration, and the St. Andrews Society of Philadelphia elected Mercer an honorary member.

Just a few weeks before Jim's call, I'd received confirmation that Mercer's "Kittanning medal," the only original example known to survive, would be loaned to *Clash of Empires* by the City of Fredericksburg, Virginia. Now Jim informed me that the St. Andrews Society owned a silver-hilted sword of French and Indian War vintage that Mercer had carried with him when he joined the American Revolutionary cause in 1775. After participating in the daring wintertime crossing of the Delaware River with his old comrade-in-arms George Washington the following year, Brigadier-General Mercer was mortally wounded during the January 3, 1777, Battle of Princeton when he refused to surrender to a group of British soldiers who had surrounded him. American artist Jonathan Trumbull immortalized the moment in a dramatic painting.

Family tradition holds that as Mercer lay dying of multiple bayonet wounds in British custody, he presented his sword to fellow French and Indian War veteran Jacob Morgan. Morgan's daughter-in-law presented it to the St. Andrews Society of Philadelphia in 1841, in appreciation for its role in reburying Mercer's remains and erecting a monument to his memory.

A dead end search for an early rifle, a sharp-eyed curator sorting through a box of family knickknacks, and a sharp-eared trustee with an interest in the French and Indian War brought Wyck's Indian pouch and Hugh Mercer's sword to *Clash of Empires.* How do curators find all that stuff you see in museum exhibitions? Happy accidents and strange coincidences play a bigger role than most of us are eager to admit.

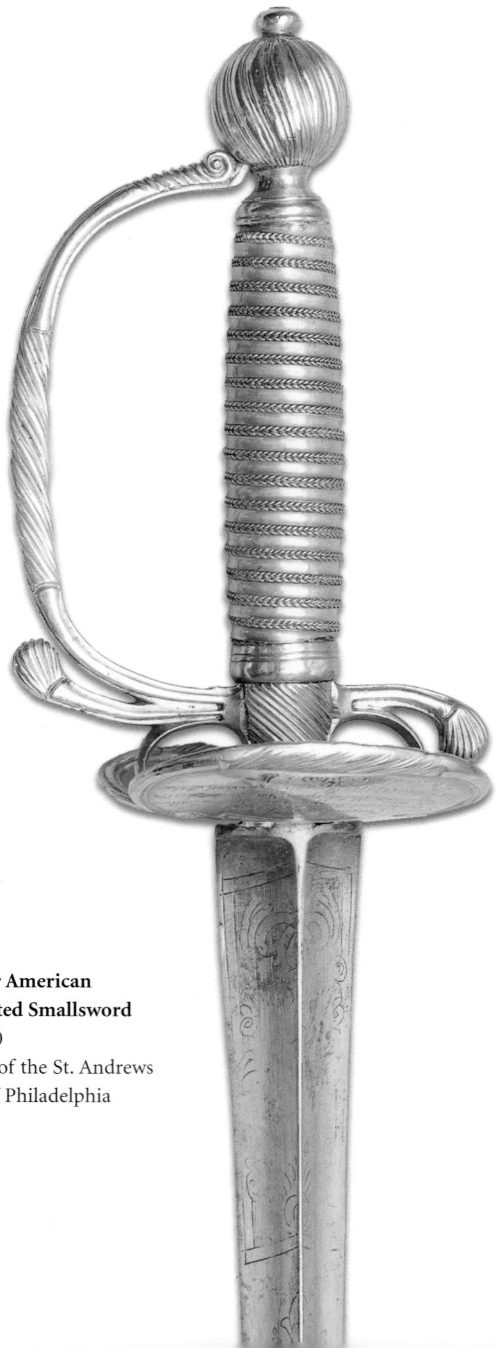

British or American Silver-hilted Smallsword
c. 1750-60
Courtesy of the St. Andrews Society of Philadelphia

The Death of General Mercer at the Battle of Princeton, 3 January, 1777
John Trumbull, c. 1789-1831
Yale University Art Gallery,
Trumbull Collection

Third in Trumbull's Revolutionary War series, this work depicts the mortal wounding of fallen Brigadier-General Hugh Mercer at the Battle of Princeton. This American victory was the last conflict in Washington's winter campaign against the British in New Jersey. Scottish immigrant Mercer (1726-1777) led Pennsylvania provincial troops in the French and Indian War, practiced medicine in Fredericksburg, Virginia, and joined the American revolutionary cause in 1775.

Senator John Heinz Regional History Center, Pittsburgh, 2005. Photograph by Ed Massery

THE MAKING OF AN EXHIBIT

Behind the Scenes of *Clash of Empires*

BY BRIAN BUTKO WITH INTERVIEWS BY PAUL PREZZARIA

THIS PUBLICATION REPRESENTS MANY OF THE ARTIFACTS found in *Clash of Empires: The British, French & Indian War, 1754-1763*, an exhibition that debuted at the Pittsburgh Regional History Center on May 1, 2005. It is the first and only comprehensive museum exhibition on the French and Indian War. After April 23, 2006, it travels to the Canadian War Museum/Museum of Civilization in Ottawa, Canada. After six months there, it will then be displayed at the Smithsonian Institution in Washington, D.C.

Dozens of people have been working behind the scenes for three years to assemble this impressive collection of art, artifacts, dioramas, videos, and historically accurate figures. Museum curators, catalogers, educators, designers, and fabricators worked with the History Center's Development, Marketing, and Library & Archives staffs to coordinate this huge undertaking. Artifacts arrived almost daily: uniforms, weapons, documents, and items that were once part of the everyday life of European, colonial, and American Indian peoples. Museum staff and volunteers spent the months leading up to the opening unpacking and registering the objects, building display cases, making artifact mounts, scanning images, and producing text and caption panels.

Peter Argentine filmed reenactors on the Allegheny River while recreating scenes from the French and Indian War for the exhibit's introductory film. ©*Richard Kelly Photography*

Curator Scott Stephenson at the History Center's new museum registration room. *Lora Hershey*

Paintings and portraits in the exhibit depict key figures, towns, and battles. Dioramas put the wilderness landscape into perspective by recreating period scenes such as a birch bark canoe being portaged by a Canadian and an Iroquois Indian, or Fort Necessity's shot-through wooden stockade. Films and videos also tell parts of the story, and custom-designed interactive stations help children to understand this important piece of American history.

In this section, you'll meet some of the craftspeople who made this exhibit not only a reality, but an absorbing, informative experience. Much of this information was gleaned from interviews conducted by Paul Prezzaria in spring 2005.

Craig Britcher works on the exhibit. *Lora Hershey*

For more than a quarter century, **J. Lee Howard** has been painting miniature soldiers and building dioramas. He began by collecting plastic soldiers and military models at age 10. He has built a following in the past decade by painting thousands of miniatures for collectors and war gamers. The museum staff at the History Center asked him to create a small diorama depicting Braddock's mortal wounding at the Battle of the Monongahela. The project has since grown to become an epic display of the entire battle, incorporating more than 600 individual soldiers, wagons, and artillery pieces. Another diorama was commissioned to depict Fort Duquesne under construction.

Howard says the first step is to make sure a diorama tells a story: "Before I even painted a figure or built a structure, the museum and I worked out what we wanted to tell visitors about the subject of the two dioramas." Research came next; the History Center's Library provided a rich variety of primary and secondary sources.

Information on the Battle of the Monongahela came from a number of sources, notably the recently published *Monongahela 1754-55* by Rene Chartrand and illustrated by Stephen Walsh. "It contains topographical maps that show the hour by hour action of Braddock's Defeat that were

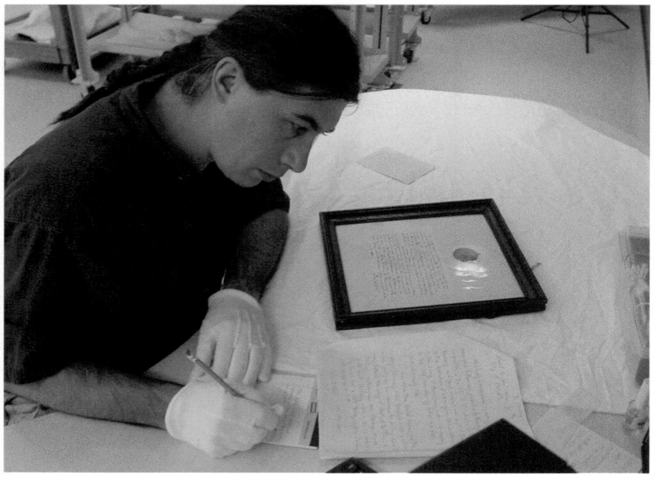

Jamie Pennisi transcribes the letter of Hugh Mercer, Jr., that accompanied the Kittanning medal. *Lora Hershey*

Lee Howard painting figures in his studio. *Courtesy of Lee Howard*

indispensable for designing the diorama. Fred Anderson's *Crucible of War* was very helpful as well. *Guns at the Forks* by Walter O'Meara was a good general source for the actions fought around the Pittsburgh area."

Fort Duquesne likewise had one outstanding resource: "I practically wore out my copy of *Drums in the Forest,* which includes "Defense in the Wilderness" by Charles M. Stotz. Not only does it include numerous eyewitness descriptions of all of the forts built at the Point, but is loaded with period maps and drawings. Stotz also authored *Outposts of the War for Empire.* It is *the* source for anyone with an interest in this subject." The History Center worked with the University of Pittsburgh to reprint both books for this anniversary.

Howard has his own library of reference materials on uniforms from various periods. A series of military dress publications from Osprey Publishing are aimed at wargamers and miniature hobbyists. But getting the colors or number of buttons right isn't always enough: "I looked at several companies and chose Pendraken Miniatures to represent the bulk of my figures. [Theirs] have personality to them as well as a wide variety of poses. The Canadian militia and Indians, for example, have many figures posed crouching or kneeling, which represents the way that they fought, taking advantage of available cover or skulking about waiting for the right moment to fire from ambush."

The Battle of the Monongahela is the more ambitious, depicting the fording of the river, the road, the profusion of trees and ground cover, and the rising ground to the right of Braddock's column. But it is not a frozen moment in time: if the diorama were accurately scaled, it would be 32 feet long and have over 3,000 figures. Instead, each figure represents five actual persons, and the areas represent different events over the four hour battle. Purists may balk, but Howard says it's aimed at a general audience: "By presenting it in this way we hope to better explain how the French and Indians, outnumbered almost two to one, were able to defeat such a superior force."

Among the more famous figures represented are General Braddock, falling back on his horse at the moment of his mortal wound. Next to him is young George Washington, reaching out from his horse to keep Braddock from toppling off of his. Two other miniatures recall a story, perhaps apocryphal, of the father/son Halketts. When Colonel Peter Halkett was hit and fell to the ground, his son James kneeled over him, was also hit, and fell across his father's body. "Both of them died in that position," says Howard. "If you look closely at the diorama, you'll see them near the line of supply wagons."

The diorama includes not only men. "Despite being ordered to stay behind, many of the soldiers' wives and sweethearts continued to march along with the column. I was fortunate to find a manufacturer who made women wearing colonial dress in that scale." Visitors will also see cannons, limbers, supply wagons, and horses, as well as trees adapted from model railroad kits. "Glue is spread on the branches and they're dipped into a container holding small pieces of shredded and dyed foam rubber to represent foliage. My wife and I literally made hundreds of trees."

One of the features of Fort Duquesne that Howard wanted to emphasize is how small and cramped it was. "I built frames for the buildings from foam core. Tiny strips of balsa wood were then glued onto the foam core frames to represent squared logs. Balsa was also used for the window frames and doorframes and the doors themselves. I topped the interior buildings with poster board covered with a pattern representing wooden shingles in raised ink similar to that used on business cards. The structures were then painted."

The model depicts the fort under construction, with workers cutting, sawing, and laying the logs, digging the dry moat surrounding the fort, and constructing stockade walls. The surrounding land includes a bakery, livestock, crops, and a small Native American village. Small pup tents, fences, and cornstalks — cast in resin — were purchased from Musket Miniatures. An arriving flotilla of canoes represents the victorious French and Indian forces returning from the skirmish at Fort Necessity.

VISITORS TO THE EXHIBIT WILL ENJOY MAPS that are new yet curiously at home among artifacts from 250 years ago. These detailed drawings are the work of **Fred Threlfall**, whose creations are historically accurate in a number of ways. He uses only materials that would have been available in their time period; for this project, that meant pencil, quill, ruler, T-Square, paper, watercolor, cotton paper, and inks such as brown-hued walnut ink. He makes the ink himself by boiling black walnuts and mixing the mash with ingredients like oil and vinegar.

Threlfall grew up just southeast of Pittsburgh in Homestead. An uncle there inspired his love of history: "He only went to third grade, but he always read afterward. We used to sit on a rock overlooking the river and Braddock's field, and he used to tell me, 'This is where they crossed' or 'this is where so-and-so was supposed to be.'" Threlfall had little training in art other than blueprint classes, but his interest and skill grew while working at Fort Necessity.

The hardest part, he says, is not making a mistake: "It's tough to erase. You have to take your time; you can't rush. And they made mistakes back then. Often they would use guidelines to keep things straight, which you can still see even if they tried to take them off."

The original mapmakers were able to be accurate, despite not having airplanes, satellites, and cameras, by using triangulation; that is, viewing or measuring the same object from two different places and then using math to determine distances. The trick then and now was to make it accurate and artistic: "What's challenging to me are the technical things; how to get on a piece of paper what is required, you know the distance and area, and have it somewhat presentable as a piece of art.... It takes a lot of head work or eye work."

Threlfall always puts a little trivia on his work to make it interesting. His favorite part is adding vignettes in the tradition of the originals. For example, the map of the Braddock campaign has an Indian pointing his tomahawk towards the site of the Battle of the Monongahela. Another portrays the difficult, 20-mile portage of canoes from Lake Erie to French Creek. Each vignette conveys a lesser-known aspect that Threlfall thought was important to tell: "One of the vignettes I have on that map is Reverend Post talking

Fred Threlfall made maps for the exhibit using period techniques.
Lora Hershey

to the Indians at the Kuskuskey. That was very important, and it was there that they turned on the French. That assisted the success of the Forbes campaign." Another scene portrays a native family, possibly from one of the French mission villages, coming to upper Ohio: "I'm sketching a family who are on their way, where maybe they'll have a better opportunity, just to show that families were moving, sometimes encouraged by the missionaries."

The first map in the exhibit depicts Native American nations in the Ohio Country as the war began. The area had been uninhabited for about 75 years due to Iroquois expansionism, then other native groups come back into the area. "That's what we're showing," says Threlfall. "How they're coming back in, and where from and how they are. And some are coming for different reasons, but they're all coming to the rich Ohio Valley. Some of the native groups figure they can get a better deal with the English than with the French, so they start moving closer to this chain of friendship that extended from the east of the Ohio Valley."

Following that is a depiction of the Trans Allegheny. "I'm showing the campaigns, first the French one, where they send a military expedition from Canada to take possession of the Ohio, then the English response first with Colonel Washington. We'll follow General Braddock, then we're going to have Armstrong in there with his attack on Kittanning in 1756, and then Forbes in 1758." Various events and battles co-exist on single maps by assigning different colors.

ONE OF THE MOST STRIKING OBJECTS early in the exhibit is a 26-foot-long canoe. It's not an artifact but an amazingly realistic recreation from the hands of **Jan Zender and Rochelle Dale**. The project took two years: the first preparing, including finding the right roots and bark, the second one building. Even the seemingly simple construction requires many complex steps when being done in a traditional manner, from steaming the cedar ribbing to bend it to collecting lots of firewood to heat the pitch.

Zender and his wife make much more than canoes; they produce Native American-style crafts from the Great Lakes region such as trade silver ornaments, wooden utensils, coats from caribou hides, clothing for historical mannequins, and canoe-related items such as paddles. They are helped by their son, 20, and daughter, 13, plus another couple, John and Victoria Jungwirth and their two children. They named their company for the Yellow Dog River, which empties into Lake Superior. From where they live and work, they can see the lake eight miles away.

All their products are made with traditional tools such as axes, butcher knives, and wooden mallets, but this is no gimmick. "There is a deep philosophical reason behind the way we live. We feel that we live in an appropriate way, making minimum impact on the earth while acting as a whole family." Their art and way of life are really intertwined. "We live in the woods, cut our own logs for our own log house, and we get most of what we need from where we live. We haul water from a spring and shoot deer for their hides. It's sort of a romantic way of life; we're not living in an apartment in some city making 'Native American art.'"

"Canoe building is the most complicated Indian art," Zender explains, "because it requires the most knowledge. You have to know quill work and how to tan a hide. You have to have knowledge of the materials, the tools. You have to work during the

Jan Zender and Rochelle Dale led the building of a canoe using 18th-century Native American methods. *Courtesy of Zender and Dale*

right seasons; for example, our wives collect the spruce roots at certain times. You need perfect bark and perfect wood." Rochelle and Victoria also take care of most of the stitching and bark-stripping.

The first step is finding bark and wood that are both free of knots. "For the bark, you need to find a straight birch tree. Then you have to find trees with bark thick enough for a canoe. You test it by peeling it back a little bit. Loggers make it hard to find trees with thick enough bark, because they're usually cut down too young. We had to look at hundreds of trees to find wood with the right grain for the ribbing."

The bark on a canoe is inside-out. The visible lines are traced by the pitch, and under the pitch are stitches holding the pieces together. Zender explains that completing the long row of stitches across the boat is very time-consuming: "You need two people, one on the inside of the canoe and one on the outside, to keep feeding the spruce root in and out of the holes. Stitching is pretty tedious anyway, and there is also a lot of time spent just splitting the spruce root in half. The preparation of the seams has the most drudgery. There is also the fact that spruce roots are collected during black fly season; that's pretty bad in itself."

Different types of wood were used for different parts of this extra-long canoe: "The gunwales are made from ash, as well as the caps and the forks. The ribbing is made from cedar, as well as the very thin layers of wood that line the floor of the canoe. The stem piece is made from basswood fiber, and of course there are the spruce roots, although they aren't exactly wood."

The pitch is found like maple syrup: by cutting trees and collecting the sap that oozes out. "We heat the sap, and then mix it with charcoal and bear fat. How much bear fat we use depends on what the canoe will be used for. More fat will keep it flexible in the winter, while using less will make it harder in the summer."

Zender's mother is French Canadian, several of her relatives married Indians, and one of her relatives was a trapper. "She would tell stories that were just great," he recalls. "Eventually, she moved to the United States, and lived in the country, where I was born."

Rochelle also grew up in the country, in the Southern U.S. "She appreciated the fact that we could have a way of earning our living from art while living this way. We spent some time in a tepee and even lived in Pine Ridge," a reservation in South Dakota.

ANOTHER ASPECT OF THE EXHIBITION that helps visitors experience the past firsthand are life-like recreations of personalities from the war. Nine figures were meticulously crafted by **Gerry Embleton** of Prêles, Bernese Jura, Switzerland. His figures can be seen in this book's sidebars, one per chapter.

Born in London, he began helping his brother Ronald with comic strips and had his first illustration published at 14. A year later, Embleton left school to freelance as an illustrator and comic strip artist. He has illustrated more than 200 books, scores of book jackets, educational artwork, and posters. He also draws and paints purely for the love of doing it, but has exhibited some of it too around the world. He points to a job in 1971 as a turning point when he illustrated *Universal Soldier*. The editor and writer, Martin Windrow, became a close friend and colleague, plus he got to work with some of the greatest experts on military costume. Afterwards, he says, "I researched and painted the uniforms worn

Courtesy of Zender and Dale

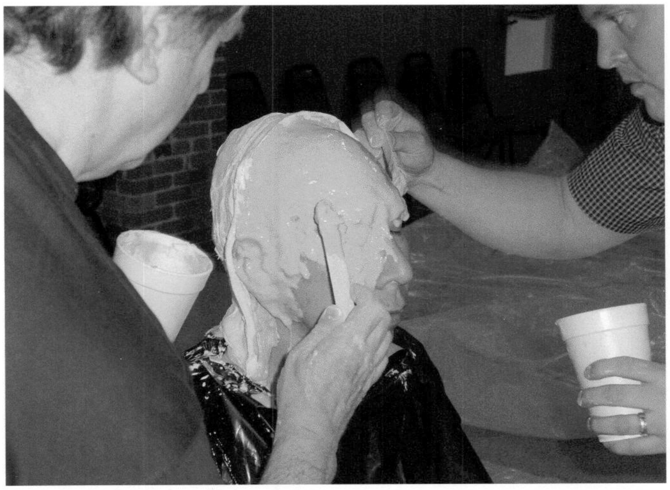

As a model for one of Embleton's figures, Paul Winnie has alginate applied by Gerry, left, and Alan Gutchess. *Lora Hershey*

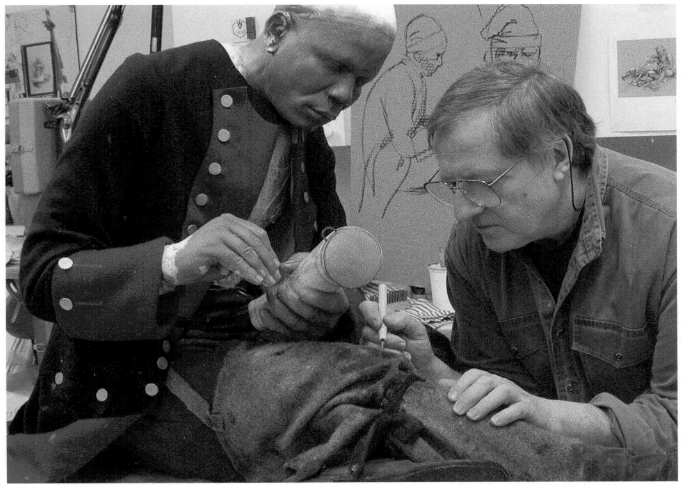

Gerry Embleton crafted nine figures for the exhibit.

during the American Revolution, which led to a consultancy for the *London Sunday Times* bicentennial exhibition at the Royal Maritime Museum and several major commissions."

Embleton is a long-time member of the Company of Military Historians (USA), the Society for Army Historical Research (GB), and the Sabretache (F). "I've illustrated more than 60 books on military costume, always emphasizing what was *actually* worn rather than regulation dress, and written and illustrated many articles on various aspects of the subject."

After moving to Switzerland in 1983, Embleton was invited to work for the Swiss Institute of arms and armour at Grandson castle, eventually rising to head of the Creative Art Department. "I made my first exhibition of three-dimensional costumed figures in a very realistic and individual style as part of the total refurbishing of the Castle of Lenzburg in Switzerland, which won a European prize. In 1988 I formed my own company, Time Machine AG." At the same time, he founded the Company of Saynte George, a Swiss-based internationally recruited living history group, widely known for the accuracy of its presentations.

Time Machine's recent work ranges from a pirate exhibition in the Bahamas, to nine life-sized dioramas at the just-opened Frazier Arms Museum in Louisville, Kentucky, and has ongoing work at the largest reconstructed Bronze Age village in Europe. Another project — a book illustrating the Seven Years' War in America from the perspective of the British redcoats — dovetails with his work for the History Center.

The nine figures he crafted can be found in eight dioramas (the first one has two people) pictured throughout this publication:

- ***The Portage:*** *An Iroquois Warrior and Canadian Militiaman at Presque Isle, 1753-54*
- ***Tanaghrisson:*** *An Ohio Iroquois Leader Warns the French, September 2, 1753*
- ***George Washington:*** *Defeat at the Great Meadows, July 3, 1754*
- ***John Bush:*** *Massachusetts Soldier at Lake George, 1756*
- ***Martin Lucorney:*** *A Hungarian Red Coat at Braddock's Defeat, July 9, 1755*
- ***Honor in Defeat:*** *An Officer of the Royal-Roussillon Regiment at Montreal, September 7, 1760*
- ***Jack Tar:*** *A British Sailor Toasts the Triumph of Britannia, 1762*
- ***Captive or Kin?:*** *A Pennsylvania Girl in the Ohio Country, 1764*

Embleton jumped at the chance to create characters of this period, and especially relished the chance to honestly depict Native Americans. "They are too often still portrayed as a sort of updated version of the cigar store Indian," he says, "or as politically correct idealized fantasies. I wanted to portray them as the real people that they were, and are still, with human faults and virtues." Embleton used living Native American models both to help capture them as accurately as possible, and to explain the project and obtain their agreement.

The costumes are made incorporating unusual details such as field adaptations to uniforms, known physical descriptions, wear and tear, and weather conditions. The basic figures are then constructed from a wide variety of materials, from bio-resins and acrylic plaster to metal and wood.

"We mold all faces, hands, and some body parts from live models, assemble, paint, cloth, and then equip them. By this time they have taken on personalities of their own and I sometimes get the feeling that *they* are telling *me* what they want to look like!"

One of the intriguing figures is John Bush, portrayed carving a powder horn. With little known, and no image available, Embleton crafted him to represent the many African Americans caught up in the conflict.

"He was 'company clerk,' literate, and artistic. Several of the beautifully decorated powder horns he made survive and the one we've shown him working on is in the exhibition. I've shown him calmly working during a pause in the march. His dress reflects the semi-uniformed state of many provincial troops. John was captured at the fall of Fort William Henry; African Americans could expect to be treated as slaves if captured by the French. He died at sea, enroute to France."

Perhaps the most intriguing piece will be a young captive girl of European descent admiring the new clothes she has received from her American Indian captors. Embleton says he and History Center staff strived to push beyond the clichés of who participated in this war: "This is a young captive at a moment of complete happiness with her adopted people. I wanted the viewer to ask, 'Will she stay, or return to her own people?' Many captives were treated very harshly indeed but many others were adopted — really adopted — and treated as one of the family." The artist didn't need to look far for a model; he had one at hand in his 9½-year-old daughter Camille.

Embleton also paints in oils; here he depicts three soldiers from the Virginia Regiment, 1755. *Courtesy of Gerry Embleton*

In all his works, Embleton strives to capture people and their embellishments as they really were: "I dig deep and I enjoy the detective work. I've worn the clothes, fired black powder, eaten the food. I look for soldiers' letters and diaries, and I try to see beyond what was supposed to have been to accurately portray people and how they lived."

© *Argentine Productions*

Cameraman Frank Caloeiro moves into position to film seneca actors (from left) Paul Winnie, Warren Skye, Allan White-Kettle (Cayuga), Elmer John, Jr., and Darwin John for the *Clash of Empires* introductory video, produced by Pittsburgh-based Argentine Productions. Curator Scott Stephenson, a production consultant for historical films and television documentaries, drew on period objects and artwork to design the authentic costumes, and even made some of the props. Dozens of Native Americans served as advisors to the project, acting as historical and cultural consultants, writing letters of support, and making some of the reproduction items that appear with Gerry Embleton's striking figures.

The Making of an Exhibit

Our Sponsors

Lead Sponsor

Mellon Financial Corporation

Benefactors

The Ford Foundation
The Grable Foundation
Institute of Museum and Library Services
National Endowment for the Humanities
NOVA Chemicals

Exhibition Patrons

Alcoa, Inc.
Nadine Bognar
Jan & Robert Barensfeld
Grace Compton
Audrey & Timothy Fisher
Miryam & Robert Knutson
Ann & Martin McGuinn
Diane & Glen Meakem
Ellen & James Walton
Rachel Walton
Farley & J.C. Whetzel

This exhibition is supported by an indemnity from the Federal Council on the Arts and the Humanities.

Fine Art Patrons

Milton & Sheila Fine

Lenders

American Antiquarian Society, Worcester, Massachusetts
Association for the Preservation of Virginia Antiquities
Douglas Angeloni
Atwater Kent Museum of Philadelphia, Pennsylvania
Gordon and Margie Barlow
The Beaverbrook Art Gallery, Fredericton, New Brunswick, Canada
Bibliotheque nationale de France, Paris
Black Watch Regimental Museum, Glasgow, Scotland
The British Library, London, England
Brooklyn Museum, Brooklyn, New York
The Anne S. K. Brown Military Collection at the John Hay Library, Brown University, Rhode Island
Canadian Museum of Civilization, Gatineau, Quebec, Canada
Canadian War Museum, Ottawa, Ontario, Canada
Carnegie Museum of Natural History, Pittsburgh, Pennsylvania
Centre County Library and Historical Museum, Bellefonte, Pennsylvania
Le Centre des archives d'outre-mer, Aix-en-Provence, France
Childs Gallery, Boston, Massachusetts
Cité / Musée du Génie, Angers, France
William L. Clements Library, University of Michigan, Ann Arbor
The Colonial Williamsburg Foundation, Williamsburg, Virginia
The Connecticut Historical Society Museum, Hartford, Connecticut
Robert Connell, Pittsburgh, Pennsylvania
Corcoran Gallery of Art, Washington, DC
Darlington Library, University of Pittsburgh, Pittsburgh, Pennsylvania
Derby Museums and Art Gallery, Derby, England
Jim and Carolyn Dresslar
The Field Museum, Chicago, Illinois
Firle Estate Trustees Settlement, London, England
Fort Ligonier Association, Ligonier, Pennsylvania
Fort Necessity National Battlefield, Farmington, Pennsylvania
Fort Pitt Society, Daughters of the American Revolution, Pittsburgh, Pennsylvania
Fort Ticonderoga Museum, Ticonderoga, New York
The City of Fredericksburg, Virginia
Steve Fuller
Gilcrease Museum, Tulsa, Oklahoma
Erik Goldstein
Robert Griffing, Pittsburgh, Pennsylvania
William H. Guthman
Heeresgeschichtliches Museum, Vienna, Austria
Heritage du Canada, Ottawa
Historic Deerfield, Deerfield, Massachusetts
Historical Society of Western Pennsylvania, Pittsburgh, Pennsylvania
Hunterian Museum at the Royal College of Surgeons, London, England
The Huntington Library, San Marino, California
Huntington Museum of Art, Huntington, West Virginia
Kungl Livrustkammaren (The Royal Armory) Stockholm, Sweden
Earl and Bonnie Lanning
Library and Archives of Canada, Ottawa, Canada
The Library Company of Philadelphia, Pennsylvania
The Library of Congress, Washington, DC
Luzerne County Historical Society, Wilkes-Barre, Pennsylvania
Mackinac State Historic Parks, Mackinac, Michigan
Mariners Museum, Newport News, Virginia
The Maryland Historical Society, Baltimore, Maryland
McCord Museum of Canadian History, Montreal, Quebec
Mead Art Museum, Amherst College, Amherst, Massachusetts
Mercer Museum of the Bucks County Historical Society, Doylestown, Pennsylvania
Moravian Historical Society, Nazareth, Pennsylvania
Mount Vernon Estate and Gardens, Mt Vernon, Virginia
Musee d'art de Joliette, Quebec, Canada
William H. Myers
National Endowment for the Arts
National Gallery of Art, Washington, DC
The National Gallery, London, England
National Gallery of Canada, Ottawa, Canada
National Maritime Museum, London, England
National Museum of the American Indian, Smithsonian Institution, Washington, DC
National Portrait Gallery, London, England
Neville Public Museum of Brown County, Green Bay, Wisconsin
The Newberry Library, Chicago, Illinois
The New-York Historical Society, New York
New York State Historical Association, Cooperstown, New York
The New York Public Library, New York
Walter O'Connor
Peter the Great Museum of Anthropology and Ethnography (Kunstkamera) of the Russian Academy of Sciences, Saint Petersburg, Russia
Philadelphia Museum of Art, Philadelphia, Pennsylvania
Public Record Office, Kew, England
James B. Richardson III
Rock Foundation, New York, New York
James E. Routh Jr.
The Royal Armouries, Leeds, Yorkshire, England
The Royal Collection, Windsor Castle, Windsor, England
Royal Ontario Museum, Toronto, Ontario, Canada
Santa Barbara Museum of Art, Santa Barbara, California
Service historique de la Marine, France
Société d'Histoire de Longueuil, Quebec, Canada
State Historical Society of Wisconsin, Madison
R. Scott Stephenson
Stewart Museum, Montreal, Canada
Stroud Museum, Stroud District Council, England
Charles Thayer
Tryon Palace Historic Sites & Gardens, New Bern, North Carolina
Valley Forge National Historic PARK, Valley Forge, Pennsylvania
Vigo County Historical Society, Terre Haute, Indiana
La Ville de Longeuil, Quebec, Canada
Virginia Historical Society, Richmond
Washington-Custis-Lee Collection, Washington and Lee University, Lexington, Virginia
West Point Museum, United States Military Academy, West Point, New York
West Overton Museums, Scottdale, Pennsylvania
Winterthur Museum, Garden & Library, Winterthur, Delaware
Wyck, Historic House and Garden, Philadelphia, Pennsylvania
Wyoming Historical & Geological Society, Wilkes-Barre, Pennsylvania
Yale University, New Haven, Connecticut

Index